LOW-GI
COOKBOOK

HAMLYN HEALTHY EATING

Over 80 recipes for weight loss

LOW-GI
COOKBOOK

LOUISE BLAIR

HAMLYN HEALTHY EATING

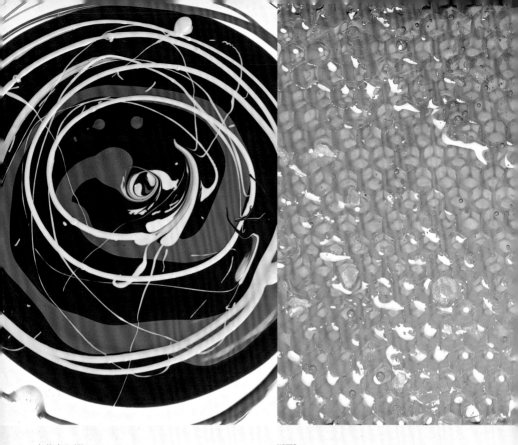

An Hachette UK company
www.hachette.co.uk

First published in Great Britain in 2005 by
Hamlyn, a division of Octopus Publishing Group Ltd
Endeavour House, 189 Shaftesbury Avenue, London WC2H 8JY
www.octopusbooks.co.uk

Revised edition 2008
This edition published in 2015

ISBN 978-0-600-63035-7

A CIP catalogue record for this book is available from the British Library.

Printed and bound in China

10 9 8 7 6 5 4 3 2 1

NOTES

Standard level spoon measures are used in all recipes
1 tablespoon = one 15 ml spoon
1 teaspoon = one 5 ml spoon

Both metric and imperial measurements are given for the recipes. Use one
set of measurements only, not a mixture of both.

Ovens should be preheated to the specified temperature. If using a fan-
assisted oven, follow the manufacturer's instructions for adjusting the time
and temperature. Grills should also be preheated.

This book includes dishes made with nuts and nut derivatives. It is advisable
for those with known allergic reactions to nuts and nut derivatives and those
who may be potentially vulnerable to these allergies, such as pregnant and
nursing mothers, invalids, the elderly, babies and children, to avoid dishes
made with nuts and nut oils. It is also prudent to check the labels of
preprepared ingredients for the possible inclusion of nut derivatives.

The Department of Health advises that eggs should not be consumed raw.
This book contains some dishes made with raw or lightly cooked eggs. It is
prudent for more vulnerable people such as pregnant and nursing mothers,
invalids, the elderly, babies and young children to avoid uncooked or lightly
cooked dishes made with eggs.

Meat and poultry should be cooked thoroughly. To test if poultry is cooked,
pierce the flesh through the thickest part with a skewer or fork – the juices
should run clear, never pink or red.

All the recipes in this book have been analysed by a professional nutritionist.
The analysis refers to each serving.

contents

INTRODUCTION

Over the following pages, you will learn about the benefits of switching to a low-GI diet. By sticking to a few simple rules, you can enjoy the many health rewards it can bring, without having to compromise on the taste or variety of your meals.

What is **GI**?

Put very simply, the glycaemic index measures how the food you eat reacts in your body. By following a low-GI diet, you choose foods that create only a positive reaction.

The majority of the foods we eat come from one main food group – carbohydrates and, more specifically, white bread, potatoes, cakes, biscuits and sugary treats. While they taste good and are easy to eat, these foods create reactions in our bodies that put the entire system out of balance. The result of this imbalance is day-to-day problems such as fatigue, mood swings and sugar cravings, plus an increased risk of a number of different health problems in the future. By basing your diet around the glycaemic index of foods, you will stop all the confusion and allow your body to develop a sense of balance, without experiencing any harmful side effects.

Fuelling your body

Your body requires a lot of energy to deal with all the stresses and strains of modern life and its preferred fuel is a sugar called glucose, which it makes from starches and sugars (carbohydrates) found in food. Glucose is made in the liver after the food has been digested in the stomach. The converted glucose is then sent to the body's cells where it is either burned immediately as we run, walk or even think, or stored in the muscles and fat stores for later use. This happens with almost every food that contains carbohydrates, whether it is a plate of spinach or a plate of doughnuts. However, different foods affect the speed with which this reaction happens and, in very basic terms, the glycaemic index is a measure of that speed. Foods with a high glycaemic index (known as high-GI foods) are converted rapidly to glucose in the body, while foods with a low glycaemic index (low-GI foods) are converted more slowly.

The missing link

A hormone called insulin provides the missing link in this process. When glucose is released into the bloodstream, insulin takes it to where it's needed. If the glucose is released slowly, moderate levels of insulin are released and have time to 'think' about where that glucose is needed most and send it there. However, if high levels of glucose enter the bloodstream, the body panics – too much glucose can be harmful. To compensate, the body releases high levels of insulin, which quickly transfer the glucose to the fat stores where it can do no harm. If this happens too often, it can lead to weight gain as well as the cells that normally respond to glucose becoming resistant to its signals. This means that less glucose is taken to where it's needed, and it remains in the bloodstream, causing cell damage, which contributes to ageing and furring of the arteries.

About turn

By switching to a low-GI diet and ensuring you eat only foods that cause a gentle rise in glucose in your bloodstream, you can reverse this process and prevent a panic reaction in your system. The results can positively affect the condition and function of every part of your body, from your heart to your skin, and will boost weight loss.

All foods are not equal

When choosing a GI eating plan, it is important that you know which foods are best to choose. There are six main elements that determine the GI of a food:

❶ Does it contain carbohydrate?
Pure protein foods such as meat, fish, poultry and eggs, and pure fats such as oils, butter and margarine, contain no carbohydrate, so the effect they have on glucose production is negligible. These foods are therefore low GI.

❷ How much starch does it contain, and in what form?
Starch is the easiest ingredient for our body to turn into glucose. In raw foods, where this starch is generally in compact particles, the body finds it difficult to break down. However, if these particles are disturbed (for example, milling into flour), the body finds it easier to digest them and therefore turns them into glucose faster.

❸ How much fibre does it contain?
Fibre makes the body break food down more slowly, which is one of the reasons why beans and pulses (which are wrapped in a fibrous shell) have such a low GI.

❹ What kind of sugar does it contain?
There are four main types of sugar. Foods high in glucose (such as sports drinks) need no

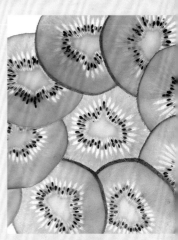

conversion, so they raise blood sugar rapidly, while fructose (the sugar in fruit) and lactose (the main sugar in dairy products) convert slowly. This gives the majority of foods containing fructose or lactose a low GI. The fourth sugar, sucrose, has a medium GI.

❺ Does it contain fat?
Fat has no effect on glucose itself, but it does slow the speed of food from the stomach to the liver, in turn slowing glucose production.

❻ How acidic is it?
Citrus fruits are an example of foods that contain acid ingredients, in this case citric acid. Other acidic ingredients include lactic acid in milk products. Acidity slows a food's progress through the system, and therefore the rate at which it converts into glucose.

GI facts about **carbohydrates**

If you follow a GI diet, the biggest changes you will probably make to your regular diet are to the following six foods: bread, breakfast cereal, grains, pasta, potatoes and rice. It is often these foods that make up the majority of our diet and they are also the easiest to convert into glucose. Don't panic though; the low-GI diet doesn't ban starchy carbohydrates. The idea is to switch your choices to those with the lowest impact on your blood sugar levels.

Bread

Many of us tend to eat a lot of bread. This is fine as long you opt for low-GI breads that are high in fibre – Granary or wholegrain are best, as the hard husk around the grains slows glucose conversion. Breads made from an ingredient with a lower GI than wheat are also a good choice. These include soya bread and rye bread.

Breakfast cereals

It's important to eat breakfast as it prevents you getting hunger pangs that lead you to eating less-nutritious snacks mid-morning. However, a high-GI breakfast cereal is just as likely to leave you hungry as having no breakfast at all. You should avoid cereals that have been processed or have high levels of added sugar or honey, and instead go for high-fibre cereals such as bran, or traditional porridge oats.

Grains

Grains are subject to minimal processing, so most have a low GI. They are also generally high in essential B vitamins and vital minerals such as magnesium or phosphorus. Barley, buckwheat, bulgar wheat, millet and quinoa (which is actually a fruit) are all low GI, while couscous is medium GI. They can all be used instead of potatoes or rice as a side dish and are also very easy and quick to prepare.

Pasta

Surprisingly, almost all pastas are low-GI foods. This is because the flour used to make them (durum wheat) contains protein, which slows its digestion. The starch particles in pasta are left fairly intact, which also slows things down. The problem with pasta is that we generally eat much larger portions than recommended, thereby increasing the amount of glucose produced. It's best to eat pasta 'al dente' – the softer the pasta, the higher its GI rating. The exception is gluten-free pasta. This is made with wheat-free flour, so doesn't have the protein protection provided by durum wheat.

Noodles

Some noodles are made from a more glutinous form of wheat flour, so are best avoided. However, glass noodles, cellophane noodles and harusame noodles are made of beans and have a very low GI rating.

Potatoes

Potatoes may be a great source of vitamin C, potassium and the anti-ageing nutrient glutathione, but they score badly on the GI plan. This is believed to be due to their high starch content, which increases if new potatoes are left on the plant to grow. In fact, new potatoes are the only potatoes to have a low GI, so choose these wherever possible, or swap potatoes for another, low-GI, carbohydrate. The other option is to use sweet potatoes, which have a medium GI and can be prepared in much the same way as regular potatoes.

Rice

The GI content of rice is dependent upon which type of starch it contains – amylose, which is tightly bonded together, or amylopectin, which is more branched out. Rices high in amylose have a lower GI.

Carbohydrate snacks

Most snacks have a high GI and even savoury snacks can raise glucose levels too quickly. However, snacking is actually encouraged on a low-GI diet, as eating a small meal or snack every two hours keeps blood sugar levels even more stable than eating three large meals a day. Try nuts, seeds, fruit, yogurt – or a little chocolate. Yes, you may be surprised to learn that chocolate has a low GI, due to a high concentration of dairy products, a high fat content and also its sucrose content, which converts into glucose at a slow rate.

GI facts about **fruit** and **vegetables**

Fruit

As a general rule, fruit is a low-GI food. The main sugar in many fruit is fructose, which has to be converted into glucose before it can be used by the body, thus preventing the sudden peak in blood sugar that can cause rapid insulin release.

What affects the GI of a fruit?

Acidity Generally, the more acidic a particular fruit is, the lower its glycaemic index.

Fibre content Fruit with the highest soluble fibre content (such as apples and pears) are those with the lowest GI.

Fructose content Most fruit contains a mixture of three sugars: fructose, sucrose and glucose. The more fructose (and less glucose) a fruit contains, the lower its GI.

Processing Canning softens the fibrous strands in fruit, making it easier to break down and slightly increasing the rate at which glucose is created. Fruit is also often canned in syrup, which can contain fast-release sugars, and raises GI from low to medium. Fruit juice also has a higher GI, as the fibre has been removed.

Vegetables

Like fruit, the majority of vegetables are low-GI foods. Despite the fact that many are classed as carbohydrate foods, the actual amount of carbohydrates they contain is very small. As well as this, most vegetables are very high in fibre, which is a GI inhibitor. There are some exceptions to this, such as starchy root vegetables (beetroot, parsnips and swede), or sweet vegetables (pumpkin), which are medium- or high-GI foods. This doesn't mean you should never eat these – as long as you keep portions moderate and don't eat them at every meal, there's no reason to entirely ban high-GI vegetables from your diet.

GI facts about **protein** foods

Pure protein foods contain no carbohydrate and so have a low GI. However, foods that contain high levels of protein, but also some level of carbohydrate, have a higher GI rating.

Beans and pulses A diet containing regular servings of legumes has been shown to lead to lower cholesterol levels, and to help balance hormones in women, possibly reducing the risk of breast cancer – so we should all be eating more of them. Most beans and pulses have a low GI due to the fibrous coating around them, which slows conversion.

Dairy products Many dairy products contain the sugar lactose, which is converted into glucose in the body. However, these sugars are converted slowly, meaning that dairy products such as milk, cheese and yogurt are low-GI foods.

Nuts and seeds The combination of protein and fats gives nuts and seeds their low GI. Some nutritionists describe seeds as a superfood and they can easily be eaten by the handful as a snack or sprinkled over salads. Remember too that spreads and dips made from nuts and seeds, such as peanut butter and tahini, will also have a low GI.

When **low**-GI meets **high**

No one wants to eat the same foods every day and the great thing about the GI eating plan is that no food is completely banned. There are, however, a few simple rules to follow when you eat a high-GI food.

The **rules**

❶ When you eat a high-GI food, watch your portion size. The more you eat of a food, the greater amounts of glucose will be produced, so if you eat less, you create less.

❷ Every time you eat a high-GI food, you should accompany it with at least two low-GI foods of the same or a larger quantity to lower the average GI of the meal. Ideally, one of the accompanying foods should be a protein food and the other should be fruit or vegetables. So, for example, if you have 25 g (1 oz) of high-GI cornflakes for breakfast, accompany this with 100 ml (3½ oz) of skimmed milk and a sliced peach.

❸ Avoid eating more than one high-GI food or two medium-GI foods in any one day – and, if at all possible, eat fewer than this. By sticking to this simple approach, you will be giving your body the chance to really get back into balance.

❹ Try to add something acidic to your meal wherever possible. In the same way that acid integrated into a food slows its conversion to glucose, so does acid added to a high-GI food. So, for example, you could eat half a grapefruit with a high-GI breakfast or accompany a main meal containing rice with a fresh side salad, topped with a vinaigrette dressing.

Low-GI portions for high-GI foods

Potatoes 100 g (3½ oz)
Rice 75 g (3 oz) cooked weight, roughly 25 g (1 oz) dried
Bread 1–2 slices
Breakfast cereals 25 g (1 oz)
Root vegetables 100 g (3½ oz)
Popcorn and pretzels 25 g (1 oz)

10 **reasons** to eat low-GI foods

❶ Your heart will thank you. According to research conducted at Harvard University, women with a high intake of refined carbohydrates have 10 per cent less good cholesterol in their bloodstream. Good cholesterol keeps the heart healthy.

❷ High levels of homocysteine are linked to heart problems and the development of Alzheimer's disease in later life. By taking simple measures, such as swapping rice for wholegrains, your levels of homocysteine can fall dramatically.

❸ A diet rich in high-GI foods may increase the risk of breast cancer. The reason is that high insulin levels trigger an increase in insulin-like growth hormones, which can encourage breast cancer cells to grow.

❹ Health experts recommend eating 25–30 g (about 1 oz) of fibre a day. A high-fibre content is a contributing factor in making a food low GI, so by increasing your intake of low-GI foods, you are more likely to achieve this. Increased fibre consumption will boost weight loss, because fibre helps sweep fat calories out of the system.

❺ Many determatologists believe that refined carbohydrates trigger inflammation of the skin, which can affect the collagen and elastin fibres that keep skin firm. So, by cutting sugary foods out of your diet, you will help yourself to look younger.

❻ Reducing insulin levels can help acne and oily skin. High insulin levels lead to the release of higher levels of androgens in the system, which trigger excess sebum production.

❼ According to the World Health Organization, the number of people suffering from diabetes will double by the year 2030. Switching to low-GI diets could cut the number of potential sufferers dramatically. A low-GI diet can also help existing diabetes sufferers to control their condition more effectively, as it can help keep blood glucose levels more stable.

❽ A low-GI diet can reduce the risk of stroke. Women who switched just one serving of refined carbohydrates to wholegrains each day cut their risk of stroke by 40 per cent, say researchers at Harvard University.

❾ Sugary foods attack your immune system. When fighting illness, the average white blood cell can destroy about 14 germs in an hour. However, when exposed to 100 g (3½ oz) of sugar, that number falls to 1.4 germs per hour, and stays that way for two hours. Low-GI eating will potentially cut the risks of ailments such as colds and flu.

❿ Many exercisers think they need high-sugar bursts to fuel their bodies, but in fact sticking to a low-GI diet throughout the majority of training actually increases endurance.

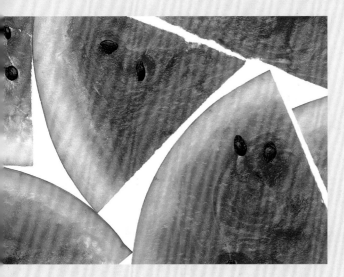

From a quick bite to a hearty meal, a good breakfast really does set you up for the day ahead. There's plenty here to suit every appetite and time constraint.

wild mushroom omelette

preparation: 10 minutes | **cooking:** 20 minutes | **serves:** 4

2 tablespoons butter

200 g (7 oz) wild mushrooms, trimmed and sliced

8 large eggs, beaten

2 tablespoons chopped parsley

50 g (2 oz) Gruyère cheese, grated

pepper

Granary toast, to serve

1 Melt a little of the butter in an omelette pan, add the mushrooms and sauté for 5–6 minutes until cooked and any moisture has evaporated. Remove the mushrooms from the pan and set aside.

2 Melt a little more butter in the same pan and add one-quarter of the beaten egg. Season well with pepper and stir with a wooden spoon, bringing the cooked egg to the centre of the pan and allowing the runny egg to flow to the edge and cook.

3 When there is only a little liquid egg left, sprinkle over a few mushrooms and some of the parsley and Gruyère, fold the omelette over and tip on to a warm serving plate. Repeat with the remaining ingredients. Serve with Granary toast.

nutritional values per serving | Kcals **282 (1172 kj)** | Protein **19 g** | Carb **0 g** | Fat **23 g**

easy corned beef hash

preparation: 10 minutes | **cooking:** 10 minutes | **serves:** 4

1 teaspoon olive oil

1 onion, chopped

350 g (11½ oz) cooked new potatoes, roughly chopped

350 g (11½ oz) corned beef, roughly chopped

1 tablespoon chopped parsley

Worcestershire sauce, to taste

pepper

thick Granary toast, to serve

1 Heat the oil in a large, nonstick frying pan. Add the onion and fry for 2–3 minutes until softened.

2 Add the potatoes and corned beef and continue to fry for 6–7 minutes, turning the mixture occasionally so that parts of it become crisp.

3 Stir through the parsley, then season to taste with Worcestershire sauce and pepper. Serve with thick Granary toast. For a change, you could also serve the hash topped with a poached egg.

nutritional values per serving | Kcals **277 (1162 kj)** | Protein **25 g** | Carb **19 g** | Fat **12 g**

creamy herby scrambled eggs on rye

preparation: 5 minutes | **cooking:** 5 minutes | **serves:** 4

8 large eggs

4 tablespoons milk

15 g (½ oz) polyunsaturated margarine

2 tablespoons light cream cheese

2 tablespoons chopped mixed tender herbs (such as parsley, oregano and chives)

salt, if liked, and pepper

4 thick slices of rye bread, to serve

1 In a bowl, beat the eggs and milk together and season with salt, if liked, and pepper. Heat the margarine in a nonstick frying pan, add the egg mixture and stir constantly with a wooden spoon for a few minutes until the eggs are softly set.

2 Remove the pan from the heat and stir in the cream cheese and herbs, then serve on thick slices of rye bread.

nutritional values per serving | Kcals **300 (1252 kj)** | Protein **19 g** | Carb **15 g** | Fat **19 g**

pear pancakes

preparation: 10 minutes | **cooking:** 20 minutes | **serves:** 4 (makes 12 small pancakes)

50 g (2 oz) polyunsaturated margarine, melted

50 g (2 oz) self-raising flour

50 g (2 oz) wholemeal self-raising flour

25 g (1 oz) oatmeal

1 tablespoon caster sugar

2 eggs, lightly beaten

275 ml (9 fl oz) buttermilk

milk, for thinning (optional)

oil, for brushing

6 pears, peeled, cored and chopped

pinch of cinnamon

1 tablespoon water

1 In a bowl, beat the margarine, flours, oatmeal, sugar, eggs and buttermilk together until smooth, adding a little milk if the mixture looks very thick.

2 Brush a nonstick frying pan with a little oil and heat. Add a ladleful of batter to the pan and cook for 2 minutes on each side until golden. Remove the pancake from the pan and keep warm. Repeat with the remaining batter mixture.

3 Meanwhile, place the pears and cinnamon in a small saucepan with the water. Cover and cook gently for 2–3 minutes until just tender. Serve the pancakes with the cooked pears.

tip

If you can't find buttermilk, mix equal quantities of natural yogurt and skimmed milk together.

nutritional values per serving | Kcals **378 (1585 kj)** | Protein **10 g** | Carb **52 g** | Fat **16 g**

buckwheat pancakes with banana and cream cheese

preparation: 10 minutes | **cooking:** 10 minutes | **serves:** 4 (makes 4 large or 8 small pancakes)

50 g (2 oz) plain flour

50 g (2 oz) buckwheat flour

300 ml (½ pint) skimmed milk

1 egg, beaten

oil, for frying

100 g (3½ oz) light cream cheese

4 small bananas, sliced

1 Sift the flours together into a bowl, tipping any bran in the sieve back into the bowl. Whisk the milk and egg together and gradually add to the flour, beating to form a smooth batter.

2 Brush a nonstick frying pan with a little oil and heat. Add a ladleful of batter to the pan and cook for 1–2 minutes on each side until golden. Remove the pancake from the pan and keep warm. Repeat with the remaining batter mixture.

3 Smooth a little cream cheese over each pancake and top with some sliced banana. Fold in half and serve.

nutritional values per serving | Kcals **276 (1160 kj)** | Protein **10 g** | Carb **43 g** | Fat **8 g**

porridge with apricot purée

preparation: 10 minutes | **cooking:** 10 minutes | **serves:** 4

175 g (6 oz) rolled oats

750 ml (1¼ pints) skimmed milk or water

2 teaspoons soft brown sugar

200 g (7 oz) ready-to-eat dried apricots

300 ml (½ pint) orange juice

1 Place the oats, milk or water and sugar in a saucepan and bring to the boil. Reduce the heat and simmer for about 10 minutes until the oats are softened and the required consistency is reached.

2 Meanwhile, place the apricots and orange juice in a separate saucepan and bring to the boil. Reduce the heat and simmer for 10 minutes. Transfer to a food processor or blender and process until smooth. Serve the purée over the porridge.

tip

As an alternative you could serve the porridge with poached fruit of your choice, such as cherries or plums.

nutritional values per serving | Kcals **344 (1460 kj)** | Protein **14 g** | Carb **66 g** | Fat **5 g**

blueberry, peach and citrus salad with wholegrain yogurt

preparation: 10 minutes | **serves:** 4

200 g (7 oz) blueberries

2 oranges, segmented

2 grapefruits, segmented

2 peaches, halved, stoned and sliced

50 g (2 oz) toasted wholegrains

300 g (10 oz) natural yogurt

2 teaspoons maple syrup

1 Divide the prepared fruit between 4 bowls. Mix the remaining ingredients together and spoon over the fruit. Serve.

tip

If you can't find wholegrains in your local health-food shop or supermarket, you can replace them with toasted mixed nuts.

Oranges are a good source of **folates**. These are essential to a baby's development in the womb and for the formation of red blood cells in adults. All citrus fruits are **high in vitamin C** as well, which **helps fight infection.**

nutritional values per serving | Kcals **183 (775 kj)** | Protein **7 g** | Carb **38 g** | Fat **1 g**

toasted fruity muesli

preparation: 10 minutes | **serves:** 4

100 g (3½ oz) jumbo oats,
toasted

25 g (1 oz) wheatgerm

25 g (1 oz) toasted mixed seeds
(such as pumpkin, sunflower and
sesame)

15 g (½ oz) hazelnuts, toasted
and roughly chopped

50 g (2 oz) ready-to-eat dried
apricots

50 g (2 oz) dried cranberries

3 dried figs, chopped

semi-skimmed milk, to serve

1 Simply combine all the
ingredients in a large mixing
bowl and serve in bowls with
semi-skimmed milk.

tip

This muesli is also
delicious served with
natural yogurt and
chopped fresh fruit, such
as pears and apples, or
summer berries.

nutritional values per serving | Kcals **293 (1237 kj)** | Protein **9 g** | Carb **48 g** | Fat **9 g**

dried fruit compôte

preparation: 5 minutes, plus standing | **cooking:** 10 minutes | **serves:** 4

450 g (14½ oz) mixed ready-to-eat dried fruit of your choice (such as apricots, figs, prunes and cranberries)

1 cinnamon stick

1 star anise

2 cardamom pods

200 ml (7 fl oz) water

100 ml (3½ fl oz) apple juice

natural yogurt, to serve

1 Place all the ingredients in a saucepan and bring to the boil. Reduce the heat, cover and simmer for 10 minutes. Remove from the heat and set aside for at least 30 minutes. Serve with natural yogurt.

nutritional values per serving | Kcals **218 (930 kj)** | Protein **4 g** | Carb **51 g** | Fat **1 g**

super smoothies
basic smoothie mixture

preparation: 5 minutes | **serves:** 1

1 small banana

150 ml (¼ pint) low-fat natural yogurt

200 ml (7 fl oz) skimmed milk

few drops of vanilla essence

nutritional values per serving
| Kcals **226 (956 kj)** | Protein **15 g** | Carb **40 g** | Fat **2 g**

1 Whizz all the ingredients together in a food processor or blender until smooth. Serve in a tall glass.

tropical fruit smoothie

1 Add the flesh of ½ ripe mango to the Basic Smoothie Mixture ingredients. Whizz all the ingredients together in a food processor or blender until smooth, then stir through the flesh of 1 passion fruit. Serve in a tall glass.

nutritional values per serving
| Kcals **276 (1160 kj)** | Protein **16 g** | Carb **51 g** | Fat **2 g**

summer berry smoothie

1 Add 75 g (3 oz) mixed summer berries (thawed if frozen) to the Basic Smoothie Mixture ingredients. Whizz all the ingredients together in a food processor or blender until smooth. Serve in a tall glass.

nutritional values per serving
| Kcals **247 (1036 kj)** | Protein **16 g** | Carb **43 g** | Fat **2 g**

apple and oat smoothie

1 Add 1 peeled, cored and chopped apple, 2 teaspoons clear honey and 2 tablespoons muesli to the Basic Smoothie Mixture ingredients. Whizz all the ingredients together in a food processor or blender until smooth. Serve in a tall glass.

nutritional values per serving
| Kcals **415 (1750 kj)** | Protein **19 g** | Carb **80 g** | Fat **4 g**

Lunch on the go doesn't have to mean a sandwich. These recipes are all quick to prepare, or they can be cooked while you're doing other things. Being busy is all the more reason to have a lunch that you can look forward to.

summer vegetable soup

preparation: 10 minutes | **cooking:** 15 minutes | **serves:** 4

1 teaspoon olive oil

1 leek, finely sliced

1 large potato, chopped

450 g (14½ oz) mixed summer vegetables (such as peas, asparagus, broad beans and courgettes)

2 tablespoons chopped mint

900 ml (1½ pints) Vegetable Stock (see below)

2 tablespoons light crème fraîche

salt, if liked, and pepper

1 Heat the oil in a medium saucepan, add the leek and fry for 3–4 minutes until softened.

2 Add the vegetables to the pan with the mint and the stock and bring to the boil. Reduce the heat and simmer for 10 minutes.

3 Transfer the soup to a food processor or blender and process until smooth. Tip back into the pan with the crème fraîche and season with salt, if liked, and pepper. Heat through and serve.

vegetable stock

preparation: 10 minutes | **cooking:** 1½ hours | **makes:** about 1.2 litres (2 pints)

1 tablespoon olive oil

1 onion, chopped

1 carrot, chopped

4 celery sticks, chopped

any vegetable trimmings (such as celery stalks, onion skins and tomato skins)

1 bouquet garni

1.7 litres (2¾ pints) water

salt and pepper

1 Heat the oil in a large saucepan, add the vegetables and trimmings and fry for 2–3 minutes. Add the bouquet garni and season well with salt and pepper. Add the water and bring to the boil. Reduce the heat and simmer gently for 1½ hours. Strain.

nutritional values per serving | Kcals **136 (566 kj)** | Protein **6 g** | Carb **17 g** | Fat **5 g**

corn chowder

preparation: 15 minutes | **cooking:** 25 minutes | **serves:** 4

1 teaspoon olive oil

1 onion, chopped

450 g (14½ oz) potatoes, chopped

600 ml (1 pint) Vegetable Stock (see page 32)

300 ml (½ pint) milk

1 bay leaf

325 g (11 oz) can sweetcorn kernels, drained

2 large tomatoes, chopped

2 tablespoons chopped parsley

salt, if liked, and pepper

1 Heat the oil in a medium saucepan, add the onion and fry for 2–3 minutes until beginning to soften. Add the potatoes and continue to fry for 2 minutes, then add the stock, milk and bay leaf. Bring to the boil, then reduce the heat and simmer gently for 15 minutes.

2 Add the sweetcorn and tomatoes and continue to simmer for 5 minutes, then remove the bay leaf. Transfer the soup to a food processor or blender and process until smooth. Return to the pan with the parsley and season with salt, if liked, and pepper. Heat through and serve.

nutritional values per serving | Kcals **265 (1123 kj)** | Protein **8 g** | Carb **50 g** | Fat **5 g**

chicken and pearl barley broth

preparation: 15 minutes | **cooking:** 35 minutes | **serves:** 4

1 teaspoon oil

2 leeks, finely sliced

1 carrot, chopped

1 celery stick, chopped

250 g (8 oz) lean boneless, skinless chicken, finely sliced

25 g (1 oz) pearl barley, prepared and cooked according to pack instructions

900 ml (1½ pints) Chicken Stock (see below)

2 tablespoons chopped parsley

salt, if liked, and pepper

1 Heat the oil in a medium saucepan, add the leeks, carrot and celery and fry for 3–4 minutes until beginning to soften. Add the chicken and continue to fry for 2 minutes. Add the barley and stock and bring to the boil. Reduce the heat and simmer for 20 minutes.

2 Transfer half the soup to a food processor or blender and process until smooth. Return to the pan with the parsley and season well with salt, if liked, and pepper. Heat through and serve.

nutritional values per serving | Kcals **122 (513 kj)** | Protein **15 g** | Carb **8 g** | Fat **3 g**

chicken stock

preparation: 5–10 minutes | **cooking:** about 2½ hours | **makes:** about 1 litre (1¾ pints)

cooked chicken carcass

raw giblets and trimmings

1 onion, chopped

2 carrots, chopped

1 celery stalk, chopped

1 bay leaf

a few parsley stalks, lightly crushed

1 sprig of thyme

1.8 litres/3 pints water

1 Chop a cooked chicken carcass into 3 or 4 pieces and place it in a large saucepan with the other ingredients. Bring to the boil, removing any scum from the surface. Lower the heat and simmer for 2–2½ hours. Strain and cool before refrigerating.

cauliflower and cumin soup

preparation: 10 minutes | **cooking:** 20 minutes | **serves:** 4

1 teaspoon oil

1 onion, chopped

1 garlic clove, crushed

1 teaspoon cumin seeds

1 cauliflower, cut into florets

1 large potato, chopped

450 ml (¾ pint) **Vegetable Stock** (see page 32)

450 ml (¾ pint) milk

2 tablespoons light crème fraîche

2 tablespoons chopped fresh coriander

salt, if liked, and pepper

1 Heat the oil in a medium saucepan, add the onion, garlic and cumin seeds and fry for 3–4 minutes. Add the cauliflower, potato, stock and milk and bring to the boil. Reduce the heat and simmer for 15 minutes.

2 Transfer to a food processor or blender and process until smooth. Stir through the crème fraîche and coriander and season with salt, if liked, and pepper. Heat through and serve.

tip

This is delicious served with multigrain bread, topped with melted Gruyère cheese.

Used extensively in Middle Eastern and Indian cooking, **cumin seeds** were traditionally believed to be **good for the digestive system** and science has since backed up this claim. To release the aroma and flavour, cumin seeds should always be roasted or fried.

nutritional values per serving | Kcals **152 (640 kj)** | Protein **8 g** | Carb **19 g** | Fat **6 g**

gazpacho

preparation: 15 minutes, plus chilling | **serves:** 4

1 thick slice of day-old white bread

2 tablespoons white wine vinegar

450 g (14½ oz) ripe tomatoes, skinned and chopped

1 garlic clove, crushed

300 ml (½ pint) passata

300 ml (½ pint) water

few drops of Tabasco sauce

1 small red pepper, cored, deseeded and chopped

½ cucumber, chopped

½ red onion, finely chopped

handful of basil, torn

1 tablespoon extra virgin olive oil

salt, if liked, and pepper

1 Tear the bread into pieces and soak in the vinegar. Place the tomatoes, garlic, passata, soaked bread and water in a food processor or blender and process until smooth. Season with salt, if liked, and pepper, and add Tabasco to taste.

2 Cover and chill in the refrigerator for at least 1 hour. Serve the soup topped with a mixture of the pepper, cucumber, onion and basil, then drizzle over a little oil.

nutritional values per serving | Kcals **123 (520 kj)** | Protein **5 g** | Carb **20 g** | Fat **4 g**

aubergine and chickpea pâté

preparation: 10 minutes | **cooking:** 10 minutes | **serves:** 4

1 tablespoon olive oil

1 aubergine, chopped

200 g (7 oz) can chickpeas, drained and rinsed

100 g (3½ oz) light cream cheese

3 spring onions, finely sliced

2 tablespoons chopped mixed herbs (such as parsley, basil and chives)

salt, if liked, and pepper

to serve

crudités

toasted wholemeal pitta bread

1 Heat the oil in a nonstick saucepan, add the aubergine and fry for 7–8 minutes until tender. Don't add any more oil as this is plenty. Leave to cool.

2 Transfer the aubergine to a food processor or blender with all the remaining ingredients and process until almost smooth but retaining a little texture. Serve the pâté with crudités and toasted pitta bread.

nutritional values per serving | Kcals **140 (588 kj)** | Protein **7 g** | Carb **11 g** | Fat **8 g**

herby griddled haloumi on bulgar and beetroot salad

preparation: 15 minutes, plus standing and cooling | **cooking:** 10 minutes | **serves:** 4

4 tablespoons chopped mixed herbs

grated rind and juice of 1 lemon

1 tablespoon toasted hazelnuts

1 tablespoon olive oil

100 g (3½ oz) haloumi cheese, cut into 8 slices

150 g (5 oz) bulgar wheat

2 cooked beetroot, thinly sliced

65 g (2½ oz) mixed salad leaves

grated rind and juice of 1 orange

2 teaspoons clear honey

1 teaspoon Dijon mustard

1 Place the herbs, lemon rind and juice, hazelnuts and oil in a food processor or blender and process until almost smooth but retaining a little texture. Pour over the haloumi slices and set aside for 10 minutes.

2 Heat a griddle until hot. Lay the marinated haloumi slices on the griddle and cook for 1–2 minutes on each side until beginning to brown.

3 Prepare the bulgar wheat according to the pack instructions. Leave to cool, then stir through the beetroot and salad leaves. In a small bowl, whisk the orange rind and juice, honey and mustard together, then drizzle over the bulgar and stir to combine. Serve the bulgar salad topped with the haloumi.

Beetroot is packed full of useful vitamins and minerals, including **vitamin B6, iron, calcium** and **potassium**. It can help you fight off infection and has also been credited as a possible **anti-cancer food**.

nutritional values per serving | Kcals **297 (1240 kj)** | Protein **11 g** | Carb **37 g** | Fat **13 g**

chicken and vegetable salad with a peanut dressing

preparation: 15 minutes | **serves:** 4

400 g (13 oz) carrots, coarsely grated

400 g (13 oz) white or Savoy cabbage, shredded

2 lean boneless, skinless chicken breasts, cooked and sliced

100 g (3½ oz) bean sprouts

dressing

4 tablespoons peanut butter

8 tablespoons coconut milk

1 fresh red chilli, finely chopped

2 tablespoons chopped fresh coriander

flour tortillas or pitta bread, to serve

1 In a large bowl, mix all the salad ingredients together. In a small bowl, whisk all the dressing ingredients together.

2 Drizzle the dressing over the salad and toss together. Serve the salad with flour tortillas or pitta bread, to make a tasty wrap or sandwich.

nutritional values per serving | Kcals **277 (1157 kj)** | Protein **25 g** | Carb **17 g** | Fat **12 g**

eggs baked with spinach and ham

preparation: 10 minutes | **cooking:** 15 minutes | **serves:** 4

175 g (6 oz) baby spinach leaves

1 tablespoon water

100 g (4 oz) sliced ham, chopped

1 tomato, sliced into 4

4 eggs

4 tablespoons light crème fraîche

40 g (1½ oz) mature Cheddar cheese, grated

salt, if liked, and pepper

multigrain bread, to serve

1 Place the spinach in a saucepan with the water and heat gently for 2–3 minutes until the spinach is wilted.

2 Divide the spinach between 4 mini pudding basins or dariole moulds, top with ham and a tomato slice, then crack an egg into each. Spoon a tablespoon of crème fraîche over each, sprinkle with Cheddar and season with salt, if liked, and pepper.

3 Place on a baking sheet and bake in a preheated oven, 200°C (400°F), Gas Mark 6, for 10 minutes until the eggs are just set. Serve with multigrain bread to dip in the juices.

nutritional values per serving | Kcals **178 (740 kj)** | Protein **14 g** | Carb **2 g** | Fat **13 g**

blue cheese soufflés with chicory and walnut salad

preparation: 25 minutes | **cooking:** 10–12 minutes | **serves:** 4

25 g (1 oz) polyunsaturated margarine

50 g (2 oz) plain flour

300 ml (½ pint) milk

4 eggs, separated

100 g (3½ oz) Stilton cheese, crumbled

1 teaspoon chopped thyme

oil, for oiling

4 heads of chicory, leaves separated

handful of watercress

1 tablespoon walnuts, toasted

2 tablespoons fat-free dressing

pepper

1 Melt the margarine in a medium saucepan, add the flour and stir over the heat for 1 minute. Gradually add the milk, whisking constantly, and cook until thickened.

2 Remove from the heat and beat in the egg yolks, one at a time. Stir in the Stilton and thyme and season well with pepper. In a large, clean bowl, whisk the egg whites until they form firm peaks. Gradually fold them into the cheese mixture.

3 Transfer to 4 lightly oiled ramekins and bake in a preheated oven, 190°C (375°F), Gas Mark 5, for 10–12 minutes until risen and golden. Toss the remaining ingredients together and serve with the soufflés.

Walnuts are a great source of **potassium** and **vitamin E,** as well as being **rich in beneficial omega-3 and omega-6 oils**. Store them in the refrigerator or in a cool, dry place in an airtight container to keep fresh.

nutritional values per serving | Kcals **360 (1505 kj)** | Protein **18 g** | Carb **16 g** | Fat **26 g**

new potato, watercress and bacon salad

preparation: 10 minutes, plus standing | **cooking:** 20 minutes | **serves:** 4

900 g (1 lb 13 oz) baby new
potatoes, scrubbed

4 lean back bacon rashers,
chopped

2 tablespoons olive oil

1 teaspoon Dijon mustard

juice of 1 lemon

1 teaspoon clear honey

150 g (5 oz) watercress, roughly
chopped

2 heads of red chicory or
radicchio, cut into bite-sized
pieces

pepper

1 Cook the potatoes in a
saucepan of boiling water for
12–15 minutes until tender. Drain
and tip into a serving bowl.

2 Cook the bacon in a dry,
nonstick pan for 3–4 minutes
until crisp. Add the oil, mustard,
lemon juice and honey and
stir well. Tip into the bowl with
the potatoes, mix together
and set aside for 30 minutes.
Stir through the remaining
ingredients and season well
with pepper. Serve.

nutritional values per serving | Kcals **260** (1096 kj) | Protein **10 g** | Carb **39 g** | Fat **9 g**

turkey and avocado salad with toasted seeds

preparation: 10 minutes | **serves:** 4

450 g (14½ oz) cooked turkey, sliced

1 large avocado, sliced

2 red apples, cored and sliced

1 punnet of mustard cress

125 g (4 oz) mixed salad leaves

50 g (2 oz) toasted mixed seeds (such as pumpkin and sunflower)

dressing

3 tablespoons apple juice

3 tablespoons low-fat natural yogurt

1 teaspoon clear honey

1 teaspoon wholegrain mustard

wholegrain rye bread, to serve

1 In a large bowl, toss all the salad ingredients together. In a separate bowl, whisk all the dressing ingredients together.

2 Pour the dressing over the salad, mix together well and serve with slices of wholegrain rye bread.

nutritional values per serving | Kcals **372 (1557 kJ)** | Protein **39 g** | Carb **15 g** | Fat **18 g**

bulgar wheat salad with fennel, orange and spinach

preparation: 10 minutes, plus cooling | **cooking:** 15 minutes | **serves:** 4

150 g (5 oz) bulgar wheat

2 tablespoons olive oil

2 fennel bulbs, finely sliced

175 g (6 oz) baby spinach leaves

3 oranges, segmented

2 tablespoons pumpkin seeds, toasted

dressing

4 tablespoons natural yogurt

2 tablespoons chopped fresh coriander

½ small cucumber, finely chopped

salt, if liked, and pepper

1 Prepare the bulgar wheat according to the pack instructions. Set aside to cool. Heat half the oil in a frying pan, add the fennel and fry for 8–10 minutes until tender and browned. Add the spinach to the pan and stir through until just wilted.

2 Toss through the bulgar wheat, then the orange segments and pumpkin seeds. Mix all the dressing ingredients together with the remaining oil, stir through the salad and serve.

nutritional values per serving | Kcals **296 (1237 kj)** | Protein **10 g** | Carb **44 g** | Fat **9 g**

low-fat chicken Caesar salad

preparation: 15 minutes | **cooking:** 10 minutes | **serves:** 4

4 small chicken breasts

1 tablespoon olive oil

2 cos lettuces, chopped

½ cucumber, sliced

croûtons

4 slices of wholegrain bread

1 garlic clove, halved

dressing

3 tablespoons light crème fraîche

1 anchovy fillet, chopped

grated rind and juice of ½ lemon

2 tablespoons freshly grated Parmesan cheese

salt, if liked, and pepper

1 Brush the chicken breasts with a little of the oil and season well with pepper. Heat a griddle until hot, lay on the chicken breasts and cook for 3–4 minutes on each side until cooked through. Slice each chicken breast.

2 Divide the lettuce and cucumber between 4 serving plates and top each with a sliced chicken breast.

3 To make the croûtons, drizzle the remaining oil over the bread and grill until toasted on each side. Rub all over with the cut sides of the garlic, cut the toast into cubes and add to the salad.

4 Blend all the dressing ingredients together and drizzle over the salad. Serve.

nutritional values per serving | Kcals **279 (1170 kj)** | Protein **28 g** | Carb **18 g** | Fat **11 g**

tortilla pizza

preparation: 10 minutes | **cooking:** 10 minutes | **serves:** 4

4 medium flour tortillas

4 tomatoes, thinly sliced

2 pears, peeled, cored and thinly sliced

100 g (3½ oz) Gorgonzola cheese, or other blue cheese, crumbled

4 tablespoons light crème fraîche

65 g (2½ oz) rocket

pepper

1 Place the tortillas on a baking sheet (or two if needed). Layer the tomatoes, pears and Gorgonzola over the tortillas, spoon over the crème fraîche and season with pepper.

2 Cook in a preheated oven, 220°C (425°F), Gas Mark 7, for 10 minutes until the cheese is bubbling. Scatter over the rocket and serve.

nutritional values per serving | Kcals **274 (1150 kj)** | Protein **10 g** | Carb **35 g** | Fat **11 g**

homemade hummus with roasted vegetables in tortillas

preparation: 10 minutes | **cooking:** 45 minutes | **serves:** 4

400 g (13 oz) can chickpeas, drained and rinsed

1 garlic clove

2 tablespoons Greek yogurt

juice of 1 lemon

pinch of paprika

1 aubergine, cut into batons

1 red pepper, cored, deseeded and sliced

2 courgettes, sliced

2 carrots, cut into batons

1 red onion, sliced

1 tablespoon olive oil

1 teaspoon chopped thyme

8 small flour tortillas

1 Place the chickpeas, garlic, yogurt, lemon juice and paprika in a food processor or blender and process until smooth. Tip into a bowl, cover and set aside.

2 Place the vegetables in a roasting tin, drizzle over the oil and sprinkle over the thyme. Cook in a preheated oven, 200°C (400°F), Gas Mark 6, for 45 minutes until tender and beginning to char.

3 Meanwhile, warm the tortillas according to the pack instructions, then fill with the roasted vegetables and hummus and serve.

High in fibre and **protein, chickpeas,** along with lentils and other legumes, are particularly beneficial to a vegetarian diet. However, as the fibre they contain can also **help reduce cholesterol,** we should all be eating more of them.

nutritional values per serving | Kcals **422 (1783 kj)** | Protein **16 g** | Carb **74 g** | Fat **9 g**

poached eggs with lentils and rocket

preparation: 10 minutes | **cooking:** 45 minutes | **serves:** 4

250 g (8 oz) Puy lentils

450 ml (¾ pint) Vegetable Stock
(see page 32)

1 teaspoon olive oil

4 spring onions, finely sliced

3 tomatoes, chopped

125 g (4 oz) rocket

4 eggs

salt, if liked, and pepper

1 Place the lentils and stock in a medium saucepan and bring to the boil. Reduce the heat and simmer for about 40 minutes until tender. Drain off any excess liquid.

2 Heat the oil in a frying pan, add the spring onions and tomatoes and fry for 2 minutes. Stir through the lentils and rocket and season with salt, if liked, and pepper.

3 Bring a large saucepan of lightly salted water to the boil, then reduce to a very gentle simmer and crack in one of the eggs. Swirl the water very gently to wrap the white around the yolk and cook for 3 minutes. Remove the egg from the pan and repeat with the remaining eggs. Serve on top of the lentils and rocket.

nutritional values per serving | Kcals **304 (1284 kj)** | Protein **24 g** | Carb **33 g** | Fat **10 g**

creamy mushroom medley on Granary

preparation: 10 minutes | **cooking:** 10 minutes | **serves:** 4

1 tablespoon olive oil

1 garlic clove, crushed (optional)

750 g (1½ lb) mixed mushrooms (such as flat cap, oyster and cep), trimmed and sliced

1 tablespoon wholegrain mustard

2 tablespoons light crème fraîche

2 tablespoons chopped parsley

4 thick slices of Granary toast

1 Heat the oil in a large frying pan, add the garlic, if liked, and fry for 1 minute. Add the mushrooms and sauté for 5–6 minutes until tender.

2 Stir in the mustard, crème fraîche and parsley and bring to the boil. Remove from the heat and serve on the Granary toast.

nutritional values per serving | Kcals **206 (869 kj)** | Protein **9 g** | Carb **27 g** | Fat **7 g**

spinach, butter bean and ricotta frittata

preparation: 10 minutes | **cooking:** 10 minutes | **serves:** 2

1 teaspoon olive oil

1 onion, sliced

400 g (13 oz) can butter beans, drained and rinsed

200 g (7 oz) baby spinach leaves

4 eggs, beaten

50 g (2 oz) ricotta cheese

salt, if liked, and pepper

tomato and onion salad, to serve

1 Heat the oil in a medium frying pan, add the onion and fry for 3–4 minutes until softened. Add the butter beans and spinach and heat gently for 2–3 minutes until the spinach has wilted.

2 Pour over the eggs, then spoon over the ricotta and season with salt, if liked, and pepper. Cook until almost set, then place under a hot grill and cook for 1–2 minutes until golden and set. Serve with a tomato and onion salad.

nutritional values per serving | Kcals **417 (1748 kj)** | Protein **32 g** | Carb **34 g** | Fat **18 g**

lentil and sweetcorn fritters with salsa

preparation: 10 minutes | **cooking:** 10 minutes | **makes:** 16–20 fritters (serves 4)

100 g (3½ oz) small green lentils

3 eggs, beaten

150 ml (¼ pint) milk

150 g (5 oz) self-raising flour

handful of fresh coriander, chopped

3 spring onions, sliced

1 fresh red chilli, chopped

325 g (11 oz) can sweetcorn kernels, drained

2 tablespoons olive oil

150 g (5 oz) Tomato Salsa (see right)

1 Prepare and cook the lentils according to the pack instructions, then drain and set aside to cool. In a bowl, beat the eggs, milk and flour together and stir in the drained lentils, coriander, spring onions, chilli and sweetcorn.

2 Heat a little of the oil in a nonstick frying pan and add tablespoons of the mixture to the pan. Fry for 1–2 minutes on each side until golden, then continue with the remaining mixture. Serve with the Tomato Salsa. The fritters are also great served with a little light crème fraîche and smoked salmon.

tip

If you prefer, you could use the same quantity of prepared and cooked split peas instead of the lentils.

tomato salsa

preparation: 10 minutes, plus standing | **serves:** 4

450 g (1 lb) cherry tomatoes, chopped

1 red onion, finely chopped

grated rind and juice of 1 lime

1 fresh green chilli, finely chopped

handful of fresh coriander, chopped

salt, if liked, and pepper

1 Simply combine all the ingredients in a large, non-metallic bowl, cover and allow the flavours to develop for about 30 minutes.

nutritional values per serving | Kcals **438** (**1852 kj**) | Protein **19 g** | Carb **66 g** | Fat **13 g**

sautéed chicken livers with wilted baby spinach

preparation: 5 minutes | **cooking:** 10 minutes | **serves:** 4

1 tablespoon olive oil

1 garlic clove, crushed

1 teaspoon chopped thyme

450 g (14½ oz) chicken livers

175 g (6 oz) baby spinach leaves

1 tablespoon balsamic vinegar

pepper

4 thick slices of Granary bread, toasted, to serve

1 Heat the oil in a medium frying pan, add the garlic and fry for 1 minute. Add the thyme and chicken livers to the pan and fry for 2–3 minutes.

2 Stir in the spinach and balsamic vinegar and cook for 1–2 minutes until the spinach has wilted. Season with pepper and serve on Granary toast.

nutritional values per serving | Kcals **318 (1340 kj)** | Protein **28 g** | Carb **27 g** | Fat **12 g**

DELECTABLE DINNERS

This range of recipes shows just how flexible following a low-GI eating plan really is. Whether it's quick after-work meals or something a bit special, look no further.

lamb with braised lentils

preparation: 15 minutes | **cooking:** 35 minutes | **serves:** 4

4 lean lamb steaks

grated rind and juice of 1 lemon

1 tablespoon chopped rosemary

1 garlic clove, crushed

2 lean smoked back bacon rashers, chopped

2 onions, sliced

1 carrot, finely chopped

1 celery stick, finely chopped

250 g (8 oz) green or Puy lentils

450 ml (¾ pint) Vegetable Stock (see page 32)

1 Rub the lamb steaks with the lemon rind, rosemary and garlic, and squeeze over the lemon juice. Heat a large, nonstick frying pan until hot, add the lamb steaks and fry for 1 minute on each side.

2 Remove the lamb from the pan. Add the bacon, onions, carrot and celery to the pan and fry for 2–3 minutes until beginning to soften. Add the lentils and stock, then return the lamb to the pan and bring to the boil. Reduce the heat and simmer gently for 30–40 minutes until the lentils are tender and most of the stock is absorbed.

nutritional values per serving | Kcals **492 (2073 kj)** | Protein **50 g** | Carb **38 g** | Fat **17 g**

braised lamb with fruity pilaf

preparation: 10 minutes | **cooking:** about 2 hours | **serves:** 4

4 lamb shanks, about 200 g
(7 oz) each

12 small rosemary sprigs

4 garlic cloves, each cut into
3 slices

1 teaspoon olive oil

2 onions, cut into wedges

600 ml (1 pint) lamb or beef
stock

200 g (7 oz) long-grain rice

12 ready-to-eat dried apricots

4 dried figs, halved

pepper

seasonal vegetables, to serve

1 Make 3 deep incisions into
each lamb shank and insert a
rosemary sprig and a piece of
garlic into each incision. Season
well with pepper.

2 Heat the oil in a large,
flameproof casserole, add the
lamb shanks and onions and fry
for 4–5 minutes, turning, until
browned all over. Pour over the
stock and bring to the boil.
Reduce the heat, cover and
simmer very gently for 1½ hours
until the meat is tender.

3 Add the rice and fruit to the
pan, cover and cook for 10–12
minutes until the stock is
absorbed and the rice is cooked.
Serve with seasonal vegetables.

beef stock

preparation: 15 minutes | **cooking:** about 4½ hours | **makes:** about 1.5 litres (2½ pints)

750 g/1½ lb shin of beef, cubed

2 onions, chopped

2–3 carrots, chopped

2 celery sticks, chopped

1 bay leaf

1 bouquet garni

4–6 black peppercorns

1.8 litres/3 pints water

½ teaspoon salt

1 Place all the ingredients
in a large saucepan. Slowly
bring to the boil, and
immediately reduce the heat
to a slow simmer. Cover
and simmer for 4 hours,
removing any scum from the
surface. Strain.

High in fibre and **vitamin C, apricots** are good for **boosting your immune system** and easing constipation. They also make a great snack.

nutritional values per serving | Kcals **599 (2518 kj)** | Protein **39 g** | Carb **79 g** | Fat **15 g**

lemon grass chicken with wok-fried vegetables

preparation: 15 minutes, plus soaking | **cooking:** about 10 minutes | **serves:** 4

18 lemon grass stalks

8 boneless, skinless chicken thighs

1 garlic clove

2 lime leaves

2 tablespoons soy sauce

1 teaspoon sesame oil

1 red pepper, cored, deseeded and sliced

1 green pepper, cored, deseeded and sliced

350 g (12 oz) sugar snap peas

2 pak choi, quartered lengthways

1 Place 16 of the lemon grass stalks in a bowl of water and leave to soak for 1 hour. Chop the remaining 2 stalks.

2 Place the chicken, chopped lemon grass, garlic, lime leaves and half the soy sauce in a food processor and process until well combined. Divide the mixture into 16 portions and mould each portion around a piece of the soaked lemon grass.

3 Place on a baking sheet, drizzle with half the oil and cook under a hot grill for 4–5 minutes, turning occasionally, until golden and cooked through.

4 Heat the remaining oil in a wok or frying pan, add the vegetables and stir-fry for 2–3 minutes until just tender, then add the remaining soy sauce. Serve the stir-fried vegetables with the chicken.

nutritional values per serving | Kcals **190 (805 kj)** | Protein **25 g** | Carb **9 g** | Fat **7 g**

stuffed chicken with sautéed greens and seeds

preparation: 10 minutes | **cooking:** 30 minutes | **serves:** 4

4 large boneless, skinless chicken thighs

75 g (3 oz) mozzarella cheese, cut into 4 slices

25 g (1 oz) toasted walnuts, chopped

2 tablespoons chopped parsley

8 ready-to-eat dried apricots, chopped

2 teaspoons olive oil

50 g (2 oz) pancetta, finely chopped

1 Savoy cabbage, shredded

25 g (1 oz) mixed seeds (such as pumpkin, sesame and sunflower)

1 Open out the chicken thighs, then beat a little to flatten slightly. Lay a piece of mozzarella on each chicken piece. Mix the walnuts, parsley and apricots together and divide between the chicken pieces. Roll up each chicken piece and secure with a cocktail stick.

2 Heat half the oil in a nonstick frying pan, add the chicken and fry for 2–3 minutes, turning, until browned all over. Place the chicken on a baking sheet and bake in a preheated oven, 200°C (400°F), Gas Mark 6, for 20 minutes until cooked through and the cheese begins to ooze.

3 Meanwhile, heat the remaining oil in a pan. Add the pancetta and fry for 2 minutes, then add the cabbage and mixed seeds and continue to fry for 5 minutes until the cabbage is tender. Serve with the chicken.

nutritional values per serving | Kcals **350 (1467 kJ)** | Protein **28 g** | Carb **20 g** | Fat **18 g**

baked sweet potato with griddled herb chicken

preparation: 10 minutes, plus marinating | **cooking:** about 1¼ hours | **serves:** 4

4 sweet potatoes, about 250 g
(8 oz) each

4 boneless, skinless chicken
breasts

6 tablespoons mixed herbs (such
as mint, parsley, fresh coriander
and oregano)

1 garlic clove

1 tablespoon capers

2 teaspoons clear honey

1 tablespoon Dijon mustard

1 tablespoon olive oil

4 tablespoons light cream
cheese

pepper

1 Place the potatoes on a baking sheet and cook in a preheated oven, 200°C (400°F), Gas Mark 6, for 1–1¼ hours until tender.

2 Meanwhile, cut 3 slices into the flesh of the chicken (be careful you don't cut all the way through). Place the herbs, garlic, capers, honey, mustard and a little of the oil in a food processor or blender and process until well combined. Rub this mixture over the chicken, cover and leave in the refrigerator for at least 30 minutes for the flavours to develop.

3 Heat a griddle until hot, drizzle the remaining oil over the chicken, then place the chicken on the griddle and cook for 3–4 minutes on each side until beginning to char and the chicken is cooked through.

4 Cut the sweet potatoes open, spoon in some cream cheese and season with plenty of pepper. Serve with the chicken.

nutritional values per serving | Kcals **435 (1842 kj)** | Protein **34 g** | Carb **52 g** | Fat **12 g**

griddled duck with plum confit and layered potatoes

preparation: 15 minutes | **cooking:** 1 hour | **serves:** 4

450 g (14½ oz) new potatoes, scrubbed and thinly sliced

2 garlic cloves, thinly sliced

1 teaspoon chopped thyme

2 tablespoons olive oil

150 ml (¼ pint water)

4 boneless duck breasts, skinned

4 teaspoons Chinese five-spice powder

2 large onions, sliced

1 tablespoon sugar

2 tablespoons white wine vinegar

6 plums, halved, stoned and sliced

pepper

steamed green vegetables, to serve

1 Layer the potatoes, garlic and thyme in a shallow, ovenproof dish. Mix half the oil and the water together, pour over the potatoes and season well with pepper. Cover with foil and cook in a preheated oven, 180°C (350°F), Gas Mark 4, for 1 hour until the potatoes are tender, removing the foil halfway through cooking.

2 Meanwhile, rub the skin of the duck with the five-spice powder, place on a hot griddle or in a hot frying pan and fry for 3–4 minutes on each side, draining off any excess fat.

3 Heat the remaining oil in a small saucepan, add the onions and sugar and fry for 10 minutes until caramelized. Add the vinegar and plums, season with pepper and continue to cook for a further 10 minutes.

4 Slice the duck and serve with the potatoes and plum confit, and plenty of green vegetables.

nutritional values per serving | Kcals **375 (1575 kj)** | Protein **30 g** | Carb **39 g** | Fat **12 g**

Bolognese-filled pasta shells with cheeses

preparation: 15 minutes | **cooking:** 35 minutes | **serves:** 4

1 teaspoon olive oil

1 onion, chopped

1 celery stick, chopped

1 carrot, chopped

200 g (7 oz) mushrooms, sliced

450 g (14½ oz) turkey mince

300 ml (½ pint) passata

2 tablespoons chopped parsley

16 large wholewheat pasta shells, cooked according to pack instructions

100 g (3½ oz) ricotta cheese

2 tablespoons freshly grated Parmesan cheese

pepper

salad, to serve

1 Heat the oil in a large frying pan, add the onion, celery, carrot and mushrooms and fry for 3–4 minutes until softened.

2 Add the turkey mince and continue to fry, stirring to break up, for 5 minutes until browned. Pour the passata over the mince and bring to the boil. Reduce the heat and simmer for 20 minutes. Stir through the parsley and season well with pepper.

3 Place the pasta shells in a large, ovenproof dish and divide the Bolognese mixture between them. Spoon a little ricotta on top of each, then sprinkle over the Parmesan. Bake in a preheated oven, 200°C (400°F), Gas Mark 6, for 10 minutes until golden and bubbling. Serve with a salad.

nutritional values per serving | Kcals **515 (2189 kj)** | Protein **43 g** | Carb **68 g** | Fat **10 g**

gourmet 'Greek' burgers

preparation: 10 minutes | **cooking:** about 10 minutes | **serves:** 4

450 g (14½ oz) steak mince

1 tablespoon sun-dried tomato paste

2 teaspoons chopped oregano

50 g (2 oz) feta cheese, crumbled

a little beaten egg

4 wholemeal rolls, toasted

1 red onion, sliced

1 Little Gem lettuce, leaves separated

pepper

1 In a large bowl, mix the steak mince, tomato paste, oregano and feta together. Season well with pepper, and stir through enough beaten egg to bind. Form the mixture into 4 burgers.

2 Place the burgers under a hot grill and cook for 4–5 minutes on each side until browned and cooked through. Make up the burgers in the rolls, with the onion and lettuce, and serve with a napkin.

nutritional values per serving | Kcals **324 (1364 kj)** | Protein **30 g** | Carb **27 g** | Fat **11 g**

spice-encrusted beef fillet with haricot bean mash

preparation: 10 minutes | **cooking:** 15 minutes | **serves:** 4

1 teaspoon coriander seeds

1 teaspoon cumin seeds

1 teaspoon mixed peppercorns

4 fillet steaks, about 125 g (4 oz) each

1 teaspoon olive oil

2 x 400 g (13 oz) cans haricot beans, drained and rinsed

200 ml (7 fl oz) Vegetable Stock (see page 32)

2 tablespoons light crème fraîche

2 tablespoons chopped fresh coriander

1 Place the spices in a dry frying pan and fry for 1 minute, then transfer to a mortar and roughly crush with a pestle.

2 Press the steak into the spices to cover all over. Heat the oil in the pan, add the steaks and cook for 3 minutes on each side, or until cooked to your liking.

3 Meanwhile, place the haricot beans and stock in a saucepan and bring to the boil. Reduce the heat and simmer for 10 minutes, then drain. Very lightly mash the beans together with the remaining ingredients and serve with the steak.

nutritional values per serving I Kcals **349 (1473 kj)** I Protein **37 g** I Carb **27 g** I Fat **11 g**

sticky pork steaks with pearl barley salad

preparation: 15 minutes, plus marinating | **cooking:** 20–25 minutes | **serves:** 4

4 lean pork steaks, about 150 g (5 oz) each

2 tablespoons tomato ketchup

1 tablespoon clear honey

1 teaspoon fennel seeds

1 garlic clove, crushed

2 teaspoons Worcestershire sauce

grated rind and juice of 1 orange

200 g (7 oz) pearl barley, prepared and cooked according to pack instructions

seeds of 1 pomegranate

4 spring onions, sliced

2 tablespoons chopped mint

200 g (7 oz) cherry tomatoes, quartered

1 tablespoon olive oil

1 Place the pork steaks in an ovenproof dish. Mix the ketchup, honey, fennel seeds, garlic, Worcestershire sauce and orange rind together and pour over the steaks. Turn to coat in the sauce, then cover and leave in the refrigerator for 30 minutes.

2 Drain the pearl barley, then toss through the pomegranate seeds, onions, mint, tomatoes, orange juice and oil. Cover and set aside.

3 Place the pork in a preheated oven, 220°C (425°F), Gas Mark 7, and cook for 20–25 minutes until cooked and the sauce is sticky. Serve with the salad, pouring over any excess sauce.

nutritional values per serving | Kcals **476 (2010 kj)** | Protein **36 g** | Carb **54 g** | Fat **15 g**

pan-fried pork with celeriac and potato cakes

preparation: 20 minutes | **cooking:** 15 minutes | **serves:** 4

1 tablespoon olive oil

450 g (14½ oz) pork tenderloin, cut into 1-cm (½-inch) slices

2 tablespoons dry white wine

2 teaspoons chopped sage

1 tablespoon wholegrain mustard

3 tablespoons light crème fraîche

1 head of celeriac, about 300 g (10 oz), peeled, grated and squeezed, to remove excess liquid

300 g (10 oz) new potatoes, scrubbed, grated and squeezed, to remove excess liquid

2 eggs, beaten

3 tablespoons plain flour

3 spring onions, finely sliced

pepper

steamed vegetables (such as sugar snap peas, broccoli and carrots), to serve

1 Heat a little of the oil in a frying pan. Season the pork with plenty of pepper, add to the pan and fry for 3–4 minutes until browned all over and cooked through. Remove from the pan and keep warm.

2 Pour the wine into the pan, add the sage and stir to deglaze the pan. Cook until reduced by half. Add the mustard and crème fraîche and simmer for 2 minutes. Meanwhile, in a bowl, mix the remaining ingredients, except the oil, together and form into 8 patties.

3 Heat the remaining oil in a frying pan, add the potato cakes and fry for 4–5 minutes on each side until golden, pressing down with a spatula to ensure that the mixture sticks together.

4 Place the pork on top of the potato cakes, spoon over the sauce and serve with a selection of steamed vegetables.

nutritional values per serving | Kcals **386 (1615 kj)** | Protein **31 g** | Carb **27 g** | Fat **17 g**

chilli prawns with lime basmati

preparation: 15 minutes | **cooking:** 20 minutes | **serves:** 4

450 g (14½ oz) raw tiger prawns, peeled

2 garlic cloves, crushed

2 fresh red chillies, finely chopped

2 tablespoons chopped fresh coriander

1 teaspoon sesame oil

grated rind and juice of 2 limes (reserve 2 of the lime 'shells')

225 g (7½ oz) basmati rice, rinsed

350 ml (12 fl oz) boiling water

25 g (1 oz) creamed coconut

4 tablespoons water

25 g (1 oz) peanuts, crushed, to garnish (optional)

1 Place the prawns in a non-metallic bowl. Place the garlic, chillies, coriander, oil and half the lime rind and juice in a mortar and grind with a pestle to make a paste, or use a food processor or blender. Tip over the prawns and stir, covering the prawns with the paste.

2 Place the rice in a saucepan and pour over the 350 ml (12 fl oz) boiling water, the lime 'shells' and the remaining lime rind and juice. Bring to the boil, then reduce the heat, cover and simmer for 12–15 minutes until the liquid is absorbed and the rice is tender and fluffy.

3 Meanwhile, heat a dry frying pan until hot, then add the prawns and fry for 2–3 minutes until they just turn pink. Add the coconut and water and bring to the boil, then reduce the heat and simmer for 1 minute. Serve the prawns with the rice, sprinkling over the peanuts to garnish, if liked.

When choosing **chillies**, there's a general rule to follow: the smaller the chilli, the hotter the flavour. But with their **high vitamin C content** and **antibacterial properties,** you should definitely turn up the heat.

nutritional values per serving | Kcals **367 (1535 kj)** | Protein **26 g** | Carb **48 g** | Fat **7 g**

fragrant prawn curry

preparation: 15 minutes | **cooking:** 10 minutes | **serves:** 4

6 spring onions, chopped

1–2 fresh green chillies, halved

2 garlic cloves, crushed

2 teaspoons rapeseed oil

1 teaspoon turmeric

1 teaspoon cumin seeds

1 teaspoon ground cumin

1 teaspoon mustard seeds

1 teaspoon ground coriander

5 tomatoes, chopped

2 tablespoons water

4 tablespoons double cream

50 g (2 oz) creamed coconut, dissolved in 100 ml (3½ fl oz) boiling water

450 g (14½ oz) cooked peeled prawns

2 tablespoons chopped fresh coriander

flat bread or boiled rice, to serve

1 Place the spring onions, chilli and garlic in a mortar and grind with a pestle to make a paste, or use a food processor or blender.

2 Heat the oil in a saucepan, add the turmeric, cumin seeds, ground cumin, mustard seeds and ground coriander and fry for 1 minute. Add the spring onion paste to the pan and fry for 2–3 minutes.

3 Add the tomatoes and water to the pan and simmer for 5 minutes. Add the double cream and creamed coconut and simmer for a further 2 minutes. Stir in the prawns and fresh coriander, heat through and serve with flat bread or rice.

nutritional values per serving | Kcals **387 (1608 kj)** | Protein **28 g** | Carb **7 g** | Fat **27 g**

spaghetti with crab and lemon sauce

preparation: 10 minutes | **cooking:** 10 minutes | **serves:** 4

350 g (11½ oz) spaghetti

1 teaspoon olive oil

bunch of spring onions, sliced

2 garlic cloves, crushed

1 fresh red chilli, finely sliced

300 g (10 oz) cooked fresh white crab meat

grated rind and juice of 1 lemon

6 tablespoons light crème fraîche

salt, if liked, and pepper

salad, to serve

1 Cook the spaghetti in a large saucepan of boiling water according to the pack instructions. Drain well.

2 Heat the oil in a large frying pan, then add the spring onions, garlic and chilli and fry for 3 minutes. Add the remaining ingredients with the cooked pasta. Season with salt, if liked, and pepper and heat through. Serve with a salad.

nutritional values per serving | Kcals **459 (1944 kj)** | Protein **27 g** | Carb **68 g** | Fat **11 g**

smoked haddock and pea risotto

preparation: 10 minutes | **cooking:** 25 minutes | **serves:** 4

1 teaspoon olive oil

1 small onion, finely chopped

350 g (11½ oz) Arborio rice

1 small glass dry white wine

900 ml (1½ pints) Vegetable Stock, boiling (see page 32)

350 g (11½ oz) smoked haddock fillet, skinned and cubed

200 g (7 oz) frozen peas

2 tablespoons chopped chives

3 tablespoons freshly grated Parmesan cheese, plus extra to serve (optional)

pepper

green salad, to serve

1 Heat the oil in a large, nonstick frying pan, add the onion and fry for 2–3 minutes until beginning to soften. Stir in the rice, coating it in the oil, then pour in the wine and allow to absorb.

2 Add the stock, a ladleful at a time, allowing each amount to be absorbed before adding the next. Stir constantly. Add the haddock and peas with the last ladleful of stock and cook for a further 5 minutes until the fish flakes easily.

3 Stir in the remaining ingredients and season well with pepper. The process will take about 20 minutes. Serve with a green salad and extra grated Parmesan, if liked.

nutritional values per serving | Kcals **496 (2100 kj)** | Protein **27 g** | Carb **82 g** | Fat **7 g**

baked salmon parcels

preparation: 15 minutes | **cooking:** 10–12 minutes | **serves:** 4

4 pieces of skinless salmon fillet, about 125 g (4 oz) each

1 orange, cut into 8 slices

4 spring onions, shredded

4 tablespoons light crème fraîche

handful of basil leaves

salt, if liked, and pepper

to serve

boiled new potatoes

salad or steamed vegetables

1 Place each piece of salmon in the centre of a 25-cm (10-inch) square of foil and top each with 2 orange slices. Mix the remaining ingredients together and divide between the salmon fillets.

2 Fold up each square of foil securely to enclose the salmon. Place the parcels on a baking sheet and bake in a preheated oven, 200°C (400°F), Gas Mark 6, for 10–12 minutes. Serve the salmon with new potatoes and salad or vegetables.

nutritional values per serving | Kcals **287 (1196 kj)** | Protein **25 g** | Carb **5 g** | Fat **19 g**

linguine with rocket pesto and goats' cheese

preparation: 10 minutes | **cooking:** 10 minutes | **serves:** 4

350 g (11½ oz) linguine (or a pasta shape of your choice)

125 g (4 oz) rocket

40 g (1½ oz) toasted hazelnuts

40 g (1½ oz) Parmesan cheese, freshly grated

3 tablespoons natural yogurt

100 g (3½ oz) goats' cheese, chopped

pepper

1 Cook the pasta in a large saucepan of boiling water according to the pack instructions. Drain well.

2 Meanwhile, place the rocket, hazelnuts, Parmesan and yogurt in a food processor or blender and process until almost smooth. Toss the mixture through the pasta with the goats' cheese, to warm through, season well with pepper and serve.

nutritional values per serving | Kcals **484 (2039 kj)** | Protein **22 g** | Carb **68 g** | Fat **16 g**

Asian-marinated salmon with stir-fried rice noodles

preparation: 15 minutes, plus marinating | **cooking:** about 10 minutes | **serves:** 4

4 pieces of salmon fillet, about 125 g (4 oz) each

1 garlic clove, crushed

2.5-cm (1-inch) piece of fresh root ginger, peeled and grated

2 tablespoons soy sauce

2 tablespoons rice wine vinegar

1 tablespoon sesame oil

250 g (8 oz) medium rice noodles

200 g (7 oz) mangetout, halved lengthways

150 g (5 oz) shiitake mushrooms, trimmed and sliced

4 spring onions, sliced

100 g (3½ oz) bean sprouts

2 pak choi, quartered lengthways

1 Place the salmon in a non-metallic dish. Whisk the garlic, ginger, soy sauce, vinegar and half the oil together. Pour over the salmon, cover and set aside in a cool place for at least 10 minutes, to allow the flavours to develop.

2 Heat a griddle or a nonstick frying pan until hot, add the salmon, reserving the marinade, and cook for 2–3 minutes on each side until just cooked through. Meanwhile, cook the noodles according to the pack instructions, then drain.

3 Heat the remaining oil in a frying pan or wok, add the mangetout, mushrooms, spring onions, bean sprouts and pak choi and stir-fry for 3–4 minutes. Add the reserved marinade and the noodles to the pan, toss together and heat through. Serve topped with a piece of salmon.

nutritional values per serving l Kcals **528 (2206 kj)** l Protein **32 g** l Carb **58 g** l Fat **18 g**

tofu and tomato pasta

preparation: 10 minutes | **cooking:** 15 minutes | **serves:** 4

350 g (11½ oz) wholewheat pasta shapes

1 tablespoon olive oil

250 g (8 oz) firm tofu, cut into bite-sized cubes

6 spring onions, sliced

450 g (14½ oz) cherry tomatoes, halved

handful of basil, torn

1 garlic clove, crushed

salt, if liked, and pepper

1 Cook the pasta in a large saucepan of boiling water according to the pack instructions. Drain well.

2 Meanwhile, heat the oil in a nonstick frying pan, add the tofu and fry for 3–4 minutes until golden. Mix the remaining ingredients together and toss through the pasta with the tofu. Season with salt, if liked, and pepper and serve.

nutritional values per serving | Kcals **378 (1600 kj)** | Protein **18 g** | Carb **63 g** | Fat **8 g**

moroccan vegetable stew

preparation: 20 minutes | **cooking:** 20 minutes | **serves:** 4

2 teaspoons olive oil

2 garlic cloves, sliced

2 onions, sliced

1 aubergine, chopped

625 g (1¼ lb) sweet potatoes, chopped

1 teaspoon ground cumin

1 teaspoon ground coriander

½ teaspoon turmeric

600 ml (1 pint) Vegetable Stock (see page 32)

200 g (7 oz) green beans

400 g (13 oz) can chickpeas, drained and rinsed

4 tomatoes, chopped

350 g (11½ oz) couscous

2 tablespoons chopped mixed herbs (such as mint, parsley and fresh coriander)

grated rind and juice of 1 lemon

1 Heat the oil in a medium saucepan. Add the garlic and onions and fry for 2–3 minutes until beginning to soften. Add the aubergine and sweet potatoes and fry for 3–4 minutes, then add the spices and cook for 1 minute.

2 Pour the stock into the pan and bring to the boil. Reduce the heat and simmer for 10 minutes. Add the beans, chickpeas and tomatoes and simmer for a further 5 minutes.

3 Meanwhile, prepare the couscous according to the pack instructions. Mix the herbs into the couscous with the lemon rind and juice. Serve the couscous with the stew.

nutritional values per serving | Kcals **529 (2234 kj)** | Protein **17 g** | Carb **106 g** | Fat **7 g**

stuffed roasted peppers on herby bulgar

preparation: 15 minutes | **cooking:** 30 minutes | **serves:** 4

2 red peppers, halved, cored and deseeded

2 yellow or orange peppers, halved, cored and deseeded

16 cherry tomatoes, halved

4 tablespoons cream cheese or light crème fraîche

2 tablespoons pesto

125 g (4 oz) bulgar wheat

grated rind and juice of 1 lemon

4 tablespoons chopped mixed herbs (such as parsley, mint and oregano)

6 spring onions, sliced

2 tablespoons pine nuts

1 Place the pepper halves on a baking sheet, cut-side up. Divide the halved tomatoes between the peppers. Beat the cream cheese or crème fraîche and pesto together and spoon over the peppers.

2 Season the peppers well, then cook in a preheated oven, 200°C (400°F), Gas Mark 6, for 30 minutes until tender.

3 Meanwhile, prepare the bulgar wheat according to the pack instructions, then stir through the lemon rind and juice, herbs and spring onions. Lightly toast the pine nuts in a dry frying pan.

4 Serve the bulgar wheat with the peppers, sprinkled with the toasted pine nuts.

Improved blood circulation, a **strong immune system** and **protection against strokes, heart disease and certain cancers**; these are just some of the health benefits you could enjoy by eating **peppers**.

nutritional values per serving | Kcals **309 (1290 kj)** | Protein **11 g** | Carb **36 g** | Fat **14 g**

SWEET TREATS

If you've got a sweet tooth, don't despair – low GI is about eating sensibly while also enjoying your food. We all need a little indulgence every now and again.

plum tatin

preparation: 15 minutes, plus cooling | **cooking:** 45 minutes | **serves:** 8

50 g (2 oz) butter or
polyunsaturated margarine

50 g (2 oz) golden caster sugar

600 g (1lb 3 oz) plums (any
variety), quartered and stoned

250 g (8 oz) Shortcrust Pastry
(see below)

light crème fraîche or ice cream,
to serve

1 Place the butter or margarine
and sugar in a 22-cm (8½-inch)
fixed-base cake tin over a
medium heat and cook, stirring
constantly, for about 5 minutes
until golden.

2 Carefully arrange the plums in
the tin, skin-side down. Roll out
the pastry to fit snugly over the
top of the fruit and press down.

3 Bake in a preheated oven,
190°C (375°F), Gas Mark 5, for
about 40 minutes until the
pastry is golden and the juices
are bubbling. Cool in the tin for
10 minutes, then invert on to a
large plate and serve with a little
crème fraîche or ice cream.

shortcrust pastry

preparation: 10 minutes, plus chilling | **makes:** 325 g (11 oz)

225 g (7½ oz) plain flour

50 g (2 oz) butter or
polyunsaturated margarine,
cubed and chilled

50 g (2 oz) white vegetable fat,
cubed and chilled

3–4 tablespoons cold water

1 Sift the flour into a bowl,
add the butter or margarine
and vegetable fat and rub
into the flour using your
fingertips and a light action
until the mixture resembles
fine breadcrumbs. Add the
cold water and bring
together to form a ball. Wrap
in clingfilm and chill in the
refrigerator for 30 minutes
before using.

tip

You could use half
wholemeal flour if you
prefer, giving a pastry
with a lower GI.

nutritional values per serving | Kcals **222 (928 kj)** | Protein **2 g** | Carb **27 g** | Fat **12 g**

baked exotic fruit parcels with spiced cream

preparation: 15 minutes | **cooking:** 15 minutes | **serves:** 4

1 pineapple, prepared and cut into chunks

1 mango, peeled, stoned and chopped

2 bananas, chopped

250 g (8 oz) strawberries, halved

425 g (15 oz) can lychees, drained, a little juice reserved

2 pieces of preserved ginger, finely chopped

1 teaspoon mixed spice

4 tablespoons light crème fraîche

1 Cut 4 x 25-cm (10-inch) squares of foil. Divide the fruit between the squares, add half the ginger and drizzle over a little of the reserved lychee juice. Fold up each square of foil securely to enclose the fruit.

2 Place the parcels on a baking sheet and cook in a preheated oven, 200°C (400°F), Gas Mark 6, for 15 minutes. Mix the mixed spice, crème fraîche and remaining ginger together and serve on the hot fruit parcels.

nutritional values per serving | Kcals **230 (974 kj)** | Protein **3 g** | Carb **48 g** | Fat **4 g**

baked gooseberries with oaty topping

preparation: 10 minutes | **cooking:** 40 minutes | **serves:** 4

750 g (1½ lb) fresh gooseberries, prepared

2 tablespoons demerara sugar

4 tablespoons mascarpone cheese

25 g (1 oz) butter or polyunsaturated margarine, melted

2 tablespoons clear honey

175 g (6 oz) jumbo oats

50 g (2 oz) chopped mixed nuts

low-fat natural yogurt, to serve

1 Place the gooseberries in an ovenproof dish, sprinkle over the sugar and bake in a preheated oven, 200°C (400°F), Gas Mark 6, for 20 minutes until they are tender and oozing juice.

2 Spoon the mascarpone over the gooseberries. Mix the remaining ingredients together and spoon over the gooseberries. Return to the oven and bake for 15 minutes. Serve with natural yogurt.

tip

If fresh gooseberries are unavailable, you can substitute the same quantity of plums or rhubarb in the recipe.

nutritional values per serving | Kcals **475 (1990 kj)** | Protein **10 g** | Carb **51 g** | Fat **27 g**

cappuccino panna cotta

preparation: 10 minutes, plus cooling and chilling | **serves:** 4

300 ml (½ pint) semi-skimmed milk

50 g (2 oz) caster sugar

4 tablespoons double cream

½ teaspoon vanilla essence

2 gelatine leaves

150 g (5 oz) natural yogurt

4 tablespoons very strong cold black coffee

fresh raspberries, to serve

1 Pour the milk into a medium saucepan with the sugar, cream and vanilla essence. Bring to the boil, then remove from the heat. Soak the gelatine leaves in cold water until soft.

2 Squeeze the water from the gelatine, then stir into the milk mixture until dissolved. Leave to cool (about 15 minutes) and then stir through the yogurt and coffee and whisk until smooth.

3 Strain, then pour the mixture into 4 dariole moulds. Chill in the refrigerator for 4–6 hours until set. Remove the panna cotta from the moulds by dipping the outside of each mould into a bowl of hot water for a couple of seconds, then tip on to serving plates. Serve with fresh raspberries.

nutritional values per serving | Kcals **247 (1029 kj)** | Protein **7 g** | Carb **21 g** | Fat **16 g**

instant mixed berry frozen yogurt

preparation: 5 minutes | **serves:** 4

450 g (14½ oz) mixed frozen summer berries (such as strawberries, raspberries and blackberries)

450 g (14½ oz) light Greek yogurt

1 tablespoon icing sugar

1 Place all the ingredients in a food processor or blender and process until smooth. Serve immediately, or store in a freezerproof container in the freezer until required.

nutritional values per serving | Kcals **129 (544 kj)** | Protein **7 g** | Carb **98 g** | Fat **3 g**

grapefruit syllabub

preparation: 10 minutes | **serves:** 4

200 ml (7 fl oz) whipping cream

2 tablespoons caster sugar

200 ml (7 fl oz) light Greek yogurt

grated rind and juice of 1 grapefruit

1 grapefruit, segmented

1 In a large bowl, whip the cream with the sugar until it forms soft peaks. Fold through the yogurt and grapefruit rind and juice.

2 Divide the grapefruit segments between 4 tall glasses, then spoon over the syllabub. Serve immediately or chill in the refrigerator until required.

nutritional values per serving | Kcals **272 (1130 kj)** | Protein **4 g** | Carb **53 g** | Fat **21 g**

blackberry and apple tartlets

preparation: 15 minutes | **cooking:** 20 minutes | **serves:** 4

175 g (6 oz) puff pastry, thawed if frozen

1 dessert apple, peeled, cored and very thinly sliced

a little melted butter, for brushing

200 g (7 oz) blackberries

2 tablespoons apricot jam, warmed

yogurt or light crème fraîche, to serve

1 Cut the pastry into 4 pieces and roll each out thinly to a rectangle about 8 x 15 cm (3½ x 6 inches).

2 Mark a border around the pastry pieces, 1 cm (½ inch) from the edge. Lay the apple slices inside the marked square, brush with a little butter, then bake in a preheated oven, 200°C (400°F), Gas Mark 6, for 15 minutes. Remove from the oven, add the blackberries, then return to the oven and continue to cook for 5 minutes.

3 Remove from the oven and brush with a little apricot jam. Cool, then serve with a little yogurt or light crème fraîche.

tip

If blackberries are unavailable, you can substitute them for the same quantity of blueberries or raspberries.

Eating **blackberries** can help **boost your immune system**. They are also good for **combating memory loss** as we get older, so tuck in now and you might never forget where you left the car keys again.

nutritional values per serving | Kcals **213 (890 kj)** | Protein **3 g** | Carb **28 g** | Fat **11 g**

raspberry and passion fruit fool

preparation: 10 minutes, plus overnight chilling | **serves:** 4

200 ml (7 fl oz) light evaporated milk, chilled overnight

1 tablespoon caster sugar

450 g (14½ oz) raspberries

flesh of 2 passion fruit

1 In a large bowl, whip the evaporated milk and sugar together until the mixture is thick and fluffy.

2 Process half the raspberries in a food processor or blender until smooth, then stir into the whipped evaporated milk with the whole raspberries and the passion fruit. Spoon into serving dishes and serve.

nutritional values per serving | Kcals **98 (414 kj)** | Protein **6 g** | Carb **14 g** | Fat **2 g**

banana and chocolate microwave sponge pudding

preparation: 10 minutes | **cooking:** 5 minutes | **serves:** 4

100 g (3½ oz) butter or polyunsaturated margarine, plus extra for greasing

100 g (3½ oz) self-raising flour, plus extra for dusting

75 g (3 oz) caster sugar

2 eggs

few drops of vanilla essence

50 g (2 oz) dark chocolate drops

2 bananas, sliced

1 In a large bowl, beat the butter or margarine, flour, sugar, eggs and vanilla essence together until smooth, then fold in the chocolate drops.

2 Lightly grease and flour a 600 ml (1 pint) pudding basin, layer in the banana, then pour over the sponge mixture.

3 Cover with clingfilm, then cook in the microwave on high for 4–5 minutes. Remove the clingfilm immediately and cool in the dish for 5 minutes before turning out on to a serving plate.

nutritional values per serving | Kcals **494 (2069 kj)** | Protein **7 g** | Carb **58 g** | Fat **28 g**

fruity bread and butter pudding

preparation: 15 minutes, plus standing | **cooking:** about 30 minutes | **serves:** 4

25 g (1 oz) butter

4 thick slices of Granary bread, each cut into 4 triangles

50 g (2 oz) ready-to-eat dried apricots, chopped

4 dried figs, chopped

50 g (2 oz) sultanas

3 eggs, beaten

300 ml (½ pint) milk

100 ml (3½ fl oz) single cream

pinch of nutmeg

1 Butter the bread slices and lightly butter an ovenproof dish or pudding basin. Place a layer of bread in the base of the dish or basin and sprinkle over some of the fruit. Repeat until all the bread and fruit is used up.

tip

For a change, you could use a mixture of fresh fruit to suit your taste, or use whatever you have to hand.

2 In a bowl, whisk the remaining ingredients together and pour into the dish or basin, aiming to soak all the bread. Allow to stand for 30 minutes until all the liquid is soaked up, then bake in a preheated oven, 200°C (400°F), Gas Mark 6, for about 30 minutes until golden and risen.

nutritional values per serving | Kcals **419** (**1766 kj**) | Protein **15 g** | Carb **54 g** | Fat **18 g**

simple lemon and lime cheesecake

preparation: 10 minutes | **serves:** 4

6 oaty biscuits, roughly crushed

300 ml (½ pint) vanilla or natural yogurt

200 g (7 oz) light cream cheese

grated rind and juice of 1 lime

grated rind and juice of 1 lemon

2 tablespoons caster sugar

fresh fruit, chopped, to serve

1 Divide the biscuits between 4 serving dishes. Beat the remaining ingredients together and spoon on to the biscuits. Serve immediately with some fresh fruit of your choice.

nutritional values per serving | Kcals **287 (1208 kJ)** | Protein **10 g** | Carb **37 g** | Fat **12 g**

rich chocolate mousse

preparation: 15 minutes, plus chilling | **cooking:** 2–5 minutes | **serves:** 4

150 g (5 oz) dark chocolate

2 large eggs, separated

4 tablespoons double cream, whipped to form soft peaks

25 g (1 oz) caster sugar

to serve

fresh fruit, chopped

light crème fraîche or cream

1 Place the chocolate in a heatproof bowl and set over a saucepan of barely simmering water until melted. Alternatively, you can melt the chocolate in the microwave on high for 1–2 minutes.

2 Remove from the heat and allow to cool for a couple of minutes, then beat in the egg yolks and cream. In a clean bowl, whisk the egg whites until they form soft peaks, add the sugar and continue to whisk until stiff peaks are formed.

3 Gently fold into the chocolate mixture, then spoon into 4 tall glasses or ramekins. Chill in the refrigerator for at least 2 hours. Serve with some fresh fruit and a spoonful of light crème fraîche or cream.

nutritional values per serving | Kcals **398 (1660 kj)** | Protein **6 g** | Carb **32 g** | Fat **29 g**

BAKING

Don't be put off by the kneading and proving –
baking is a piece of cake! What's more, nothing
quite beats the smell of freshly baked bread or
a tray of warm muffins.

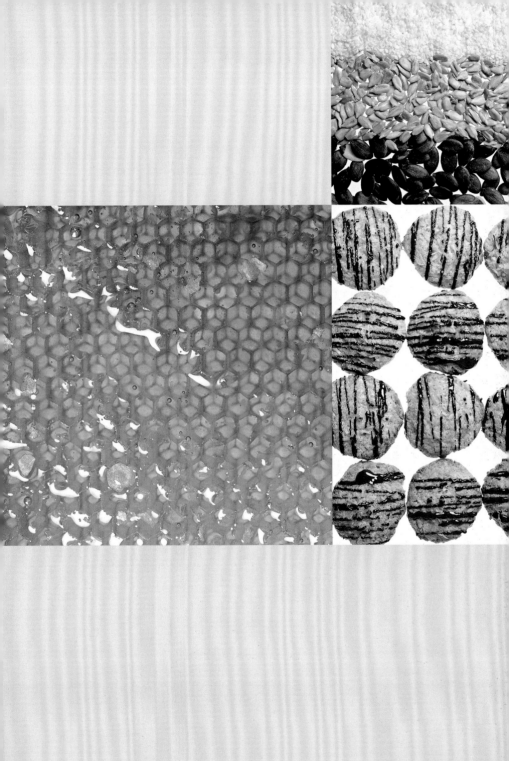

apple and apricot muffins

preparation: 20 minutes | **cooking:** 15–20 minutes | **makes:** 12

100 g (3½ oz) plain wholemeal flour

150 g (5 oz) plain flour

1 teaspoon baking powder

1 teaspoon bicarbonate of soda

2 tablespoons golden caster sugar

100 g (3½ oz) ready-to-eat dried apricots, chopped

½ teaspoon ground cinnamon

2 red dessert apples, peeled, cored and chopped

1 egg, beaten

50 g (2 oz) polyunsaturated margarine, melted

200 ml (7 fl oz) skimmed milk

1 Place 12 large muffin cases in a muffin tin. Sift the flours, baking powder and bicarbonate of soda together into a large bowl, tipping any bran in the sieve back into the bowl. Stir in the sugar, apricots, cinnamon and apples.

2 In a separate bowl, whisk the remaining ingredients together, then gently stir into the flour mixture, making sure you don't beat too much as this will spoil the end result.

3 Spoon the mixture into the muffin cases and bake in a preheated oven, 200°C (400°F), Gas Mark 6, for 15–20 minutes. Cool a little and serve.

Eating an **apple** with your lunch, or as an afternoon snack, can help stop sugar cravings. Research has also found that the fruit contains **anti-carcinogenic properties,** so all the more reason for you to enjoy an apple a day.

nutritional values per serving | Kcals **143 (603 kj)** | Protein **4 g** | Carb **24 g** | Fat **4 g**

banana bread

preparation: 15 minutes | **cooking:** 1–1¼ hours | **serves:** 12

75 g (3 oz) polyunsaturated margarine, plus extra for greasing

100 g (3½ oz) soft brown sugar

2 large eggs, beaten

3 large bananas, roughly mashed

75 g (3 oz) dates, roughly chopped

50 g (2 oz) walnuts, chopped

200 ml (7 fl oz) buttermilk

250 g (8 oz) plain wholemeal flour

1 teaspoon bicarbonate of soda

1 Lightly grease and line an 875 g (1¾ lb) loaf tin. In a large bowl, beat the margarine and sugar together until light and fluffy. Beat in the eggs, a little at a time, then stir in the bananas, dates, walnuts and buttermilk. Fold in the flour and bicarbonate of soda.

2 Spoon into the prepared tin, then bake in a preheated oven, 180°C (350°F), Gas Mark 4, for about 1–1¼ hours until a skewer comes out clean when inserted. Cool, then serve.

nutritional values per serving | Kcals **238 (1000 kj)** | Protein **6 g** | Carb **34 g** | Fat **10 g**

coconut cookies

preparation: 15 minutes, plus chilling | **cooking:** 7–8 minutes | **makes:** 18

75 g (3 oz) cornmeal (polenta)

40 g (1½ oz) plain wholemeal flour

½ teaspoon baking powder

75 g (3 oz) icing sugar

50 g (2 oz) butter, cubed and chilled

50 g (2 oz) desiccated coconut

few drops of vanilla essence

2 egg yolks

50 g (2 oz) plain chocolate

1 Line 2 baking sheets with baking parchment. In a bowl, stir the cornmeal, flour, baking powder and sugar together, then rub in the butter using your fingertips until the mixture resembles fine breadcrumbs. Stir through the coconut, then the vanilla essence and egg yolks to combine. Form into a firm dough, then roll into a sausage 5 cm (2 inches) in diameter. Wrap in clingfilm and chill in the refrigerator for 30 minutes.

2 Cut the dough 'sausage' into 18 slices and place well apart on the prepared baking sheets. Bake in a preheated oven, 180°C (350°F), Gas Mark 4, for 7–8 minutes until golden. Leave to cool on the baking sheets.

3 Break the chocolate into pieces and put them in a bowl over a saucepan of lightly simmering water until the chocolate has melted. Drizzle over the cookies using the back of a spoon.

nutritional values per serving | Kcals **97 (407 kj)** | Protein **1 g** | Carb **11 g** | Fat **6 g**

fruit and nut bars

preparation: 10 minutes | **cooking:** 15 minutes | **makes:** 8

100 g (3½ oz) butter or polyunsaturated margarine, plus extra for greasing

4 tablespoons maple syrup

2 tablespoon soft light brown sugar

150 g (5 oz) jumbo oats

100 g (3½ oz) oatmeal

50 g (2 oz) chopped mixed nuts

150 g (5 oz) mixed dried fruit (such as figs, dates, ready-to-eat apricots and cranberries), chopped

2 tablespoons sunflower seeds

1 Lightly grease and base-line a 20-cm (8-inch) square, nonstick baking tin. In a saucepan, melt the butter, syrup and sugar together. Stir in all the remaining ingredients, except the sunflower seeds, then press the mixture into the prepared tin.

2 Sprinkle over the sunflower seeds, then bake in a preheated oven, 200°C (400°F), Gas Mark 6, for 15 minutes until golden. Mark into 8 bars. Cool, then serve.

Sunflower seeds are **rich in omega-3 and omega-6** fatty acids, which can help **protect against heart disease**. They also contain the unsaturated fats that **lower blood cholesterol**, so all in all, they're a bit of a super seed! Try sprinkling them over salads or cereal.

nutritional values per serving | Kcals **368 (1542 kj)** | Protein **6 g** | Carb **46 g** | Fat **19 g**

mixed seed rolls

preparation: 20 minutes, plus proving | **cooking:** 20 minutes | **makes:** 8

450 g (14½ oz) Granary flour, plus extra for dusting

pinch of salt

7 g (¼ oz) sachet easy-blend dried yeast

100 g (3½ oz) mixed seeds (such as sesame, sunflower and pumpkin)

2 tablespoons clear honey

250 ml (8 fl oz) hand-hot water

oil, for oiling

1 In a large bowl, mix the flour, salt, yeast and the mixed seeds (reserve 1 tablespoon) together. Stir half the honey into the water, then pour into the flour and form into a soft dough.

2 Tip out on to a lightly floured surface and knead for 5 minutes. Place in a lightly oiled bowl, cover with a damp cloth and leave to prove in a warm place until doubled in size.

3 Re-knead the dough for 5 minutes, then divide into 8 pieces. Knead to form rolls, then place on a baking sheet, cover and leave to prove again until doubled in size.

4 Brush over the remaining honey and sprinkle over the reserved seeds. Bake in a preheated oven, 200°C (400°F), Gas Mark 6, for 20 minutes until the rolls are golden and sound hollow when tapped.

nutritional values per serving | Kcals **270 (1140 kj)** | Protein **10 g** | Carb **44 g** | Fat **7 g**

rye bread

preparation: 20 minutes, plus proving | **cooking:** 30–35 minutes | **makes:** 2 x 500 g (1 lb) loaves

450 g (14½ oz) strong white flour, plus extra for dusting

450 g (14½ oz) rye flour

2 x 7 g (¼ oz) sachets easy-blend dried yeast

2 teaspoons caraway seeds

1 teaspoon salt

4 tablespoons oil, plus extra for oiling

1 tablespoon clear honey

4 tablespoons low-fat natural yogurt

550 ml (17½ fl oz) tepid water

1 In a large bowl, mix the flours, yeast, caraway seeds and salt together. Stir the remaining ingredients into the water, then gradually stir into the flour mixture to form a soft dough.

2 Tip out on to a lightly floured surface and knead for 5 minutes until smooth. Place in a lightly oiled bowl, cover with a damp cloth and leave to prove in a warm place for 1 hour until doubled in size.

3 Re-knead the dough, divide into 2 pieces and shape each into an oval loaf. Place the loaves on lightly floured baking sheets, cover with a damp cloth and leave to prove again until doubled in size.

4 Slash the tops of the loaves a few times with a sharp knife, then bake in a preheated oven, 200°C (400°F), Gas Mark 6, for 30–35 minutes until golden and sounding hollow when tapped. Cool on a wire rack, then serve.

nutritional values per serving | Kcals **152** **(646 kj)** | Protein **4 g** | Carb **30 g** | Fat **3 g**

rustic nutty seed loaf

preparation: 15 minutes, plus proving | **cooking:** 30–35 minutes | **makes:** 1 large loaf

450 g (14½ oz) wholemeal flour, plus extra for dusting

1 teaspoon salt

100 g (3½ oz) mixed seeds (such as pumpkin, sunflower and poppy)

25 g (1 oz) bulgar wheat

1½ x 7 g (¼ oz) sachets easy-blend dried yeast

50 g (2 oz) mixed nuts (such as hazelnuts and walnuts), chopped

6 spring onions, sliced

50 g (2 oz) Parmesan cheese, freshly grated

1 tablespoon clear honey

300 ml (½ pint) warm water

oil, for oiling

1 In a large bowl, mix all the ingredients, except the honey and water, together. Blend the honey with the water, then stir into the flour mix and form into a dough.

2 Tip out on to a lightly floured surface and knead for 5 minutes until smooth. Place in a lightly oiled bowl, cover with a damp cloth and leave to prove in a warm place for 2 hours until doubled in size.

3 Re-knead the dough, shape into a round and place on a baking sheet. Cover with a damp cloth and leave to prove again for 1 hour. Bake in a preheated oven, 220°C (425°F), Gas Mark 7, for 30–35 minutes until it sounds hollow when tapped.

nutritional values per serving | Kcals **165** **(697 kj)** | Protein **8 g** | Carb **23 g** | Fat **7 g**

orange and sultana scones

preparation: 20 minutes | **cooking:** about 10 minutes | **makes:** 12

125 g (4 oz) self-raising flour, plus extra for dusting

100 g (3½ oz) wholemeal self-raising flour

2 teaspoons baking powder

50 g (2 oz) butter, cubed and chilled

50 g (2 oz) sultanas

1 tablespoon caster sugar

grated rind of 1 orange

1 egg

about 125 ml (4 fl oz) milk

to serve

cream cheese

fresh strawberries (optional)

1 Sift the flours and baking powder into a large bowl, tipping any bran in the sieve back into the bowl. Rub in the butter using your fingertips until the mixture resembles fine breadcrumbs, then stir in the sultanas, sugar and orange rind.

2 Break the egg into a measuring jug and beat with a fork. Make up to 150 ml (¼ pint) with milk, then pour into the flour mixture and bring together to form a soft dough, adding a little extra milk if the dough is too dry.

3 Press gently into a 1-cm (½-inch) thick round. Stamp out about 12 scones, place on lightly floured baking sheets and brush with a little milk. Bake in a preheated oven, 220°C (425°F), Gas Mark 7, for about 10 minutes, until risen and golden.

4 Cool the scones on a wire rack, then serve that day to enjoy them at their best. Serve with a little cream cheese and fresh strawberries, if liked, to bring the overall GI down.

nutritional values per serving | Kcals **120 (505 kj)** | Protein **3 g** | Carb **18 g** | Fat **4 g**

sesame seed oatcakes

preparation: 10 minutes | **cooking:** about 10 minutes | **makes:** about 12

200 g (7 oz) oatmeal

1 tablespoon sesame seeds

pinch of salt

pinch of bicarbonate of soda

1 tablespoon olive oil

2–3 tablespoons hot water

flour, for dusting

1 In a bowl, mix all the ingredients together to form a firm dough, adding a little extra water if necessary. The mixture will be very crumbly, so just keep pressing it back together.

2 Roll the mixture out on a lightly floured surface as thinly as you can. Cut out triangles or 7-cm (3-inch) rounds and place on baking sheets. Bake in a preheated oven, 180°C (350°F), Gas Mark 4, for about 10 minutes until golden and firm. Cool on a wire rack.

nutritional values per serving | Kcals **79 (330 kj)** | Protein **2 g** | Carb **11 g** | Fat **3 g**

pesto and sesame seed pastry twists

preparation: 10 minutes | **cooking:** 8–10 minutes | **makes:** 15

250 g (8 oz) Shortcrust Pastry (see page 94)

flour, for dusting

2 tablespoons pesto

2 tablespoons milk or a little beaten egg

2 tablespoons sesame seeds

1 Roll the pastry out on a lightly floured surface to a 25-cm (10-inch) square. Spoon over the pesto and smooth out, then cut the pastry into 15 strips.

2 Twist the strips and place on a baking sheet. Brush with a little milk or egg and sprinkle over the sesame seeds. Bake in a preheated oven, 200°C (400°F), Gas Mark 6, for 8–10 minutes until golden.

nutritional values per serving | Kcals **94 (390 kJ)** | Protein **2 g** | Carb **8 g** | Fat **6 g**

Parmesan and Caerphilly biscuits

preparation: 10 minutes, plus chilling | **cooking:** 10–12 minutes | **makes:** 20

125 g (4 oz) plain wholemeal flour

75 g (3 oz) butter, cubed and chilled, or polyunsaturated margarine, cut into pieces

2 tablespoons polenta

100 g (3½ oz) Caerphilly cheese, or other crumbly cheese, crumbled

50 g (2 oz) Parmesan cheese, freshly grated

50 g (2 oz) ready-to-eat dried apricots

1 egg yolk

cheese or fresh fruit (such as apples or pears), to serve

1 Sift the flour into a bowl and rub in the butter or margarine with your fingertips until the mixture resembles fine breadcrumbs. Stir in the polenta, cheeses and apricots, then add the egg yolk and bring the mixture together to form a ball. It will be very crumbly, so just keep pressing it back together.

2 Roll the ball into a sausage about 5 cm (2 inches) in diameter, wrap in clingfilm, then chill in the refrigerator for 30 minutes. Cut the dough 'sausage' into 20 slices, place on baking sheets and bake in a preheated oven, 200°C (400°F), Gas Mark 6, for 10–12 minutes until golden. Cool, then serve with cheese or fresh fruit to keep the GI down.

nutritional values per serving | Kcals **90 (373 kj)** | Protein **3 g** | Carb **6 g** | Fat **6 g**

index

acknowledgements

Executive Editor Nicola Hill
Editor Charlotte Wilson
Executive Art Editor Joanna MacGregor
Designer Ginny Zeal
Production Controller Martin Croshaw
Picture Researcher Jennifer Veall

Food Stylist Joss Herd
Photographer Gareth Sambidge